The Continued Relevance of International Humanitarian Law in the 21st Century

S-55

The Continued Relevance of International Humanitarian Law in the 21st Century

Edited by

Major General PJS Sandhu (Retd)
&
Brigadier General William Bowie (Retd)

Proceedings of a Seminar

Jointly Organised by

United Service Institution of India (USI)

And

The International Committee of the Red Cross (ICRC)

Held at
USI, New Delhi
On
11 August 2010

Vij Books India Pvt Ltd
New Delhi (India)

Published by

Vij Book India Pvt Ltd
(Publishers, Distributors and Importers)
2/19 (Second Floor), Ansari Road, Darya Ganj
New Delhi-110002 (India)
Phone : +91-11-43596460, +91-11-65449971
Fax : +91-11-47340674
web : www.vijbooks.com
Email: vijbooks@rediffmail.com

ISBN : 978-93-80177-56-4

Price in India	:	₹ 350.00
Price Outside India	:	US $ 15.00

Printed in India at Narula Printers, Delhi.

Foreword

The United Service Institution of India (USI) and the International Committee of the Red Cross (ICRC) had been in consultations regarding a joint seminar on issues of mutual concern. During a meeting held at the USI around mid 2009, the Director USI suggested that for the seminar to be meaningful, the ICRC share their experiences in some of the current hot spots of the world such as Sri Lanka, Afghanistan, etc, as well as their work with P-5 countries. Mr François Stamm, Head of the Regional Delegation (HoRD) of the ICRC in India, promised to work on this. Soon enough, he had a complete proposal with all the ingredients and thereafter things moved smoothly and quickly giving shape to the joint seminar which was held at the USI on 11 Aug 2010.

The theme selected for the seminar was "*The Continued Relevance of International Humanitarian Law (IHL) in the 21st Century*". The theme was considered most appropriate, as it is both contemporary and relevant, especially for the armed forces who willy-nilly get involved in almost all conflict situations.

The modern IHL dates back to the First Geneva Convention of 1864 and today there are almost a hundred treaties related to it. We are generally familiar with the Four Geneva Conventions of 1949 and the Two Additional Protocols of 1977. These are taught right from the time a person enters the military academy and emphasised throughout the Service Career.

India is an original signatory of the 1949 Geneva Conventions and one of the first countries to have ratified it. It gave legal sanction to IHL by enacting the Geneva Conventions Act 1960 and is also a signatory to important related international treaties and conventions like : The United Nation's Universal Declaration of Human Rights (1948), Two Additional Protocols to the Geneva Conventions (1977) etc. The solid foundation of IHL in the conduct of the Indian Armed Forces during armed conflicts is best exemplified by the humane treatment of 93,000 Pakistani Prisoners of War after the 1971 Indo-Pak War in the best traditions of the Geneva Conventions.

Yet, we cannot afford to rest on our past laurels. The nature of conflict has changed and that has given rise to fresh challenges for the armed forces who implement the State directives, the governments who authorise the use of force, and other State as well as non-State actors involved in the process. For example, the ICRC has started a project on the 60th anniversary of the 1949 Geneva Conventions that is called 'Non-International Armed Conflict Plus' (NIAC+) to address issues arising out of non-international armed conflicts. There is thus a need to keep abreast of the new challenges and the rules/conventions to meet them. To that an extent, this seminar has been most timely and relevant.

The four sessions of the seminar, were followed up with interactive discussions, during which eminent and experienced Panelists, Chairmen and knowledgeable participants, articulated their views convincingly to examine the subject threadbare. The discussants provided a deep insight into the current methods of warfare focusing, of course, on the need for protecting innocent civilians from unnecessary death, destruction and desolation, despite their being not involved in the armed conflicts.

It is equally important that the requirement of creating awareness about the IHL and connected issues of human rights, amongst the armed forces personnel and civilians is recognised and inculcated institutionally, and becomes an ongoing process. Its knowledge and best practices must spread from top to bottom as well as horizontally, and should get passed on from one generation to the next. This can be best achieved through training at various levels and different stages of an individual's service career.

This seminar saw a fairly large participation by serving officers. They will hopefully carry the message to their formations and establishments. Needless to say that this is by far the most important and difficult part of the enterprise, i.e. to institutionalise the training in IHL and human rights throughout the organisation. This seminar constituted an important step in that direction.

Finally, we wish to place on record the understanding and cooperation that existed between the USI and the ICRC during planning and conduct of the seminar.

CONTENTS

Approach Paper

Why the Seminar ?

In recent years, international humanitarian law (IHL) (the body of rules applicable in situations of armed conflict, whether international or non-international) has come to the forefront of public interest and debate. As the promoter and guardian of IHL the International Committee of the Red Cross (ICRC) welcomes the broader awareness of this important body of law. Yet, some voices have challenged the relevance of IHL to contemporary armed conflicts suggesting that it is ill equipped to deal with the threats posed to States when confronting non-state armed groups. The decades long conflict between Sri Lankan government forces and the LTTE, the protracted 10 year struggle between Nepalese government forces and the Maoists and the on-going insurgency in Afghanistan, are regional examples of such non-international armed conflicts.

An Overview

At the heart of this debate is the belief that IHL somehow places governments at a disadvantage by imposing obligations that tie their hands in the face of armed groups who are free to employ non-conventional methods of warfare to advance their goals.

The ICRC believes that this view could not be further from the truth and that the parity of rights and obligations with regards to all parties involved in the conflict is a bedrock principle of IHL. Further, IHL obligations bind both States and non-State armed groups regardless of either parties' behaviour, because IHL's primary purpose is to protect all those not involved in hostilities. As such it is the ICRC's firm belief that the primary challenge faced today is not how to revise IHL rules to make sense in modern warfare, but rather how to ensure adherence to its norms so that it can fulfil its protective function. There is also a need to take into account the experience gained in various conflict situations the world over.

Issue

Academic and military circles agree that the predominance of 21st conflicts are likely to be non-international in nature. The issue for debate is, therefore, whether IHL as a body of law is relevant in the context of these conflicts? In addition, as the ICRC continues to steadfastly believe in the application of IHL rules in all conflicts, whether international or non-international in nature, what measures are taken by the ICRC to help promote this relevance to the military and other security forces? How can the concerns of the armed forces and other security forces involved in the armed conflict be addressed without putting them at a disadvantage.

Seminar Scheme

Session I	-	Discussion regarding the relevance of IHL in a contemporary non-international armed conflict will be initiated by the Head of the Colombo Delegation of the ICRC discussing the ICRC's experiences in the recent conflict in Sri Lanka.
Session II	-	An Indian perspective of humanitarian and human rights in relation to the Indian Armed Forces will then be given by representatives of USI.
Session III	-	Using the information gained, a USI representative and the ICRC Legal advisor from the New Delhi Delegation will lead a discussion as to the applicability of IHL in contemporary armed conflicts.
Session IV	-	In conclusion, two ICRC representatives with responsibility for liaison with the armed forces will discuss the ICRC's programmes of IHL cooperation with the P5 states, focusing on the United States of America and the Russian Federation.

Participants

Lieutenant General PK Singh, PVSM,AVSM (Retd), Director, United Service Institution of India. Lieutenant General PK Singh, PVSM,AVSM (Retd) was commissioned as a 2/Lt in the Indian Army in 1967. During a military career spanning 41 years he has seen active service in the Western, Northern and North Eastern Theatres and participated in the 1971 Indo-Pak War. A graduate of the Defence Services Staff College, Wellington and the National Defence College, New Delhi, he has held several important command and staff appointments. After commanding a Corps he was appointed Director General Operational Logistics and Strategic Moves at the Army Headquarters. He was appointed C-in-C (Army Commander) in August 2006 and retired from active service in September 2008. His academic qualifications include M Sc and M Phil from the University of Madras and a Post Graduate Diploma in Business Management. He took over as Director of the United Service Institution of India, New Delhi (USI) on 1st January 2009.

Mr. François Stamm, Head of Regional Delegation, ICRC François Stamm, born on 28 November 1960 in Lausanne, Switzerland, is since September 2008 the Head of the Regional Delegation of the International Committee of the Red Cross (ICRC) in New Delhi, covering India, Bangladesh, Bhutan and Maldives. His previous posting was at the ICRC Geneva Headquarters where he held between 2002 and 2008 the position of Head of Operations for North America, Western, Central & South Eastern Europe. While in Geneva, he also held on behalf of the ICRC the position of Chair of the "Working Group on Missing Persons in Kosovo" between 2004 and 2008. Mr. François Stamm has a commercial background and is a graduate of the Lausanne Higher Business School. Following an initial career in the travel industry, he joined the International Committee of the Red Cross in 1987 and spent his first missions in South-East Asia (Cambodia, Philippines) and Africa (Zambia, Somalia, Zimbabwe, Malawi). He later focused on various operational contexts in the Balkans (Kosovo, Montenegro, Serbia, Macedonia) where he worked for eight years between 1994 and 2002. He has held various positions involving the distribution of assistance to victims of conflicts, the visits to persons deprived of freedom, contacts and negotiations with national and international representatives as well as senior operational management.

Admiral RH Tahiliani,PVSM,AVSM (Retd), Former Chief of Naval Staff. Born on 12 May, 1930 in Karachi, now in Pakistan, Admiral RH Tahiliani,PVSM,AVSM (Retd) joined the Indian Navy in March 1948. He was sent to the UK for training, qualified as a Naval Pilot and Flying Instructor in India and as Test Pilot in France. He is an alumnus of the US Naval War College, New Port and National Defence College in India. He was awarded the Ati Vishist Seva Medal in 1975 and the Param Vishist Seva Medal in 1984. He was appointed Chief of Naval Staff on -30 November 1984 and retired three years later. He was Governor of Sikkim from February 1990 upto September 1994. He is associated with Servants of the People Society, Lok Sevak Sangh and is a Member of Central Vigilance Commission Advisory Council. Currently he is the Chairman of Transparency International India. He is the Chairman of Jasbhagti Charitable Society which works for the upliftment of the weaker sections of society.

Lieutenant General AS Kalkat, SYSM, PVSM, AVSM, VSM (Retd). Commissioned in the Gurkha Regiment in 1955, he participated in Indo-Pak Wars of 1965 and 1971 and was the Commander of the Indian Peace Keeping Force in Sri Lanka. He has held the appointment of Director General, Defence Planning Staff in the Ministry of Defence and retired as GOC-in-C Southern Command in 1993. After retirement he served as became Chairman of the International Council for Conflict Resolution and has been associated with many institutions of higher learning and think tanks as a visiting faculty in India and abroad. Currently, he is the Director Emeritus, Centre for Joint Warfare Studies, New Delhi.

Mr Paul Castella, a Swiss national, was born on 04 Feb 1963. He is a Political Science (B Sc) graduate of University of Lausanne, Switzerland. He was ICRC Delegate at Kabul, Afghanistan (1993-94); ICRC Regional Disseminator of IHL to Armed Forces, Moscow, Russia (1994-1997) and ICRC Head of Section, Eastern Europe, Geneva, Switzerland (1997-99). Since then he has been the ICRC Head of Delegation at Democratic Republic of Congo (1999-2000); at Tbilisi, Georgia (2002-2005) and Amman, Jordan (2005-2008). Presently, he is the ICRC Head of Delegation Colombo, Sri Lanka, since 2008.

Lieutenant General Vijay Oberoi, PVSM, AVSM, VSM (Retd) was commissioned in 1961. A graduate of the Defence Services Staff College, Wellington, he was an International Fellow at the United States Army War College in USA in 1988-89. He has held a number of staff and instructional appointments, including the appointment of Defence Adviser at Kuala Lumpur (Malaysia). He has the rare distinction of commanding an Armoured Division, despite being an Infantry officer. He commanded a strike corps and has was the Director General Military Operations (DGMO). He was the 'Colonel' of his Regiment - The Maratha Light Infantry, for over eight years. He has commanded the Army Training Command at Shimla and the Western Command. He retired as the Vice Chief of Army Staff in September 2001. He set-up the Centre for Land Warfare Studies (CLAWS) at New Delhi, of which he was the founder Director. Presently, he takes active part in matters related to service matters, national security and welfare of ex-servicemen.

Major General Nilendra Kumar,AVSM,VSM (Retd). Major General Nilendra Kumar was the Judge Advocate General of Indian Army From Sep 2001 to Nov 2009. Born in Lucknow on 2 Nov 1949, he is a product of National Defence Academy and Indian Military Academy. He holds a law degree and diploma in Public Administration from Lucknow University and is an alumnus of Jamuna Lal Bajaj Institute of Management Studies, Mumbai. He was commissioned in the Regiment of Artillery in 1969 and took part in 1971 war in the Western Sector. He was seconded to the JAG Department in 1982. He participated in a law seminar organised by the ICRC at Geneva (1998) and attended the meetings of experts on Direct Participation of Civilians in Hostilities (2003 and 2004). He has authored / edited eleven books on military law and other subjects. He undertook concrete steps for dissemination of Human Rights among the Armed Forces personnel. Presently, he is Director of Amity Law School under Amity University, UP, NOIDA.

Lieutenant General PC Katoch, PVSM, UYSM, AVSM, SC (Retd) superannuated as Director General Information Systems of the Indian Army. A third generation army officer commissioned into The Parachute Regiment in Dec 1969, he fought in the 1971 Indo-Pak war, commanded an independent commando company in the North East, a Special Forces Unit in Sri Lanka, an Infantry Brigade on the Siachen Glacier, a Mountain Division in Ladakh and a Strike Corps in the South Western theatre. He has served as Defence Attache in Japan with accreditation to Republic of Korea. A post graduate in Defence Studies, he is an alumni of the DSSC, HC and NDC Courses. He has held staff appointments from Brigade upwards at every level in operational assignments and as ACIDS (Strategic Operations) at HQ IDS. He represented India at an International Sky Diving Competition held at Tula (USSR) in 1976. He has vast experience of operations in mountains / high altitude and in counter insurgency / counter terrorism. He is a former Colonel of The Parachute Regiment. Post retirement, he has authored numerous articles on military and security issues for professional magazines and journals.

Mr Christopher Harland is the ICRC's Regional Legal Adviser for South Asia, based in New Delhi. His responsibilities include working with governments in the region to ensure that their international obligations under international humanitarian law are reflected in their domestic legal order. Prior to his current position, he was with the Legal Division of the ICRC at its Headquarters in Geneva. A Candian lawyer, he has 12 years of experience in conflict and post-conflict environments in Africa, Europe and Asia with organisations including the ICRC and the United Nations.

Major General AJS Sandhu, VSM (Retd), was commissioned into the Regiment of Artillery on 11 Jun 1967 and retired on 31 Aug 2004. He commanded an Independent Artillery Brigade as part of a Strike Corps and has been Brigadier Incharge Administration of a Corps in J&K, during which assignment he also dealt with cases pertaining to alleged human rights violations.He attended the Higher Command Course and the National Defence College Course. He has been an instructor at various levels in the School of Artillery, Army War College, Defence Service Staff College besides having been a member of the Indian Army Training Team in Botswana. His last assignment was Additional Director General Artillery in the Army Headquarters. He has done a Post Graduate Diploma Course in International Humanitarian, Human Rights and Refugee Laws from the Indian Society of International Law, New Delhi and is now part of visiting faculty on these subjects in various civil and military institutions.

Lieutenant General Randhir Kumar Mehta, PVSM,AVSM,YSM,VSM (Retd) had a distinguished career in the Indian army. He has held numerous national command and staff positions and served as a Sector Commander with the United Nations Mission in Sierra Leone (UNAMSIL) from May 2000 to February 2001. The General has also been a member of India's delegation in various peace talks. He is a graduate of the National Defence Services Staff College, the Higher Command Course and the National Defence College. He holds Masters of Sciences and Philosophy degrees. He was honoured with the Yudh Seva Medal for gallantry in operations in Sierra Leone and the Vishisht Seva Medal. Till retirement he was a Military Adviser in the UN Department of Peacekeeping Operations (UNDPKO) in New York.

Mr Aleardo Ferretti, Senior Delegate to the Armed Forces for Canada and the United States (ICRC). Mr Aleardo Ferretti, Senior Delegate to the Armed Forces in the United States for the ICRC, joined the ICRC in 1985. His operational field experience started in Lebanon during the civil war as a field delegate and relief coordinator (until mid 1987). Later he was seconded for more than two years (1989-1992) to the ICRC operations in Sri Lanka, where he worked with the Armed Forces in creating a comprehensive Law of Armed Conflict (LoAC) training programme. More recently he spent two years (2001-2003) in Colombia as deputy head of the ICRC Delegation in Bogotâ and as the coordinator in charge of field operations and security. His last posting was in Beijing (2005-2007) where he was in charge of ICRC contacts with the Chinese, North Korean, South Korean and Mongolian armed forces. He served in the Swiss Army for over twenty years, rose through the ranks to become commander of an infantry battalion and ended his career as a Lieutenant Colonel and LoAC adviser in the staff of the Commander in Chief. Additionally he served as a UN Military Observer with UNTSO (1991-1992) on the Golan Heights and in South Lebanon. His military experience made him integrate in 1987 ICRC's newly created Unit for Relation with the Armed and Security Forces (ASF). Following various appointments as regional coordinator for ICRC's LoAC dissemination programmes with the armed forces in Europe, the Middle East and Asia, he was appointed deputy head of the ASF unit in 1993 at the ICRC headquarters in Geneva. With the decision to decentralise these activities. Mr Ferretti opened a regional ASF office in Bangkok in 1996, followed by one in Beijing in 2005, and developed LoAC dissemination activities and training programme with more than twenty armed forces in the Asia-Pacific region. He holds an MA in English Literature and Linguistics from the University of Zurich, Switzerland, and is currently the Washington based Senior Delegate to the Armed Forces for Canada and the United States.

Brigadier General William Herbert Bowie (Retd) was born on 13 January 1948 in Germistion, South Africa. He joined the South African Air Force in July 1968. After having flown various twin-engined aircraft, he was posted to C130 B Hercules aircraft at 28 Squadron at the beginning of 1972. During this tour of duty, he took part in many operations in the north of Namibia and Southern Angola. At the end of 1979, he was posted to the South African Defence Force's Military Academy where he occupied the post of Chief Military Instructor and achieved a B Mil (Honours) Degree in Geography at the University of Stellenbosch. In 1989 and 1990, he underwent Senior Command and Staff Training at the Chilean Air Force Academy in Santiago Chile. In 1994, he attended and successfully completed the South African Defence Forces Joint Staff Duties Course at the South African Defence College. He retired from the SA National Defence Force on 30 June 2002.

In February 1995, he joined the International Committee of the Red Cross (ICRC) as a Delegate to the Armed and Security Forces of the Russian Federation, the countries of the Southern Caucasus, as well as Belarus, Moldova and Ukraine. After nearly four and a half years in this post, he took up the appointment as ICRC Regional Delegate to the Armed Forces of India and Bangladesh at the end of October 2009.

Inaugural Session-Opening Remarks

HoRD of the ICRC in India

The Eminent Chairmen

Session I - The ICRC Experience in Sri Lanka

Session II - Human Rights and the Indian Armed Forces - The Chairman

Session III - IHL as Applicable in the 21st Century

Session IV - 21st Century IHL Integration into the Armed Forces - The P 5 Countries Experience (Focusing on the USA and the Russian Federation)

Concluding Remarks by HoRD of the ICRC in India and the Director, USI of India

The Continued Relevance of International Humanitarian Law in the 21st Century

Inaugural Session

Welcome Remarks	–	Lt Gen PK Singh, PVSM,AVSM (Retd), Director USI
Opening Remarks	–	Mr François Stamm, HoRD of the ICRC in India
Keynote Address	–	Admiral RH Tahiliani, PVSM,AVSM (Retd), Former CNS and Governor of Sikkim

Welcome Remarks

❑ **Lieutenant General PK Singh,PVSM,AVSM (Retd)**

Director, USI

Admiral RH Tahiliani, Mr François Stamm, distinguished chairpersons and panelists, members of the USI, participants and invitees, Ladies and Gentlemen.

It is my privilege and honour to welcome you to the joint USI-ICRC Seminar on a topic of global interest, "The Continued Relevance of International Humanitarian Law in the 21st Century"; please mark the words "Continued Relevance". I must specially thank our outstation panelists who have travelled from all over the country to participate in this seminar.

Why the seminar with the ICRC on the subject of 'The Continued Relevance of IHL in the 21st Century' ? India was one of the first countries to have ratified the four Geneva Conventions. By enacting the Geneva Convention Act it brought IHL into its domestic statutes. The humane treatment of over 90,000 Pak prisoners of war bears testimony to India's commitment to the Geneva Conventions. IHL and human rights continue to be prime concerns of the armed forces; more so, in the 21st Century. USI since its foundation in 1870 has had strong linkages with the Indian Armed Forces. It is only natural that a subject of this nature should get discussed at the USI. As the ICRC is the only institution explicitly named under IHL as a controlling authority, it is only appropriate that we are conducting this seminar jointly with the ICRC. More importantly, the seminar also gives us a chance to know how the ICRC works internationally and get to know how they interact in the field as also with other Armed Forces in the world. I would like to thank Mr François Stamm, Head of the Regional Delegation (H0RD) of the ICRC in India and Brigadier General William Bowie, Regional Delegate to the Armed Forces and Security Forces in India for their active cooperation in organising this seminar. They have undertaken more than their share of work and have addressed all our concerns.

We have four working sessions today. The first is on "IHL and Laws of Armed Conflict with regard to 21st Century Conflicts — ICRC Experience in Sri Lanka" chaired by Lieutenant General AS Kalkat who was the IPKF Commander in Sri

Lanka and later an Army Commander. The second is on "Human Rights and the Indian Armed Forces" chaired by Lieutenant General Vijay Oberoi a former VCOAS. The third is on "IHL as applicable in the 21st Century" chaired by Mr François Stamm, Regional Head of the ICRC, and the fourth is on "21st Century IHL integration into the Armed Forces: The P5 Countries experience with specific focus on the USA and the Russian Federation" chaired by Lieutenant General RK Mehta who has been the Military Advisor to the UN Secretary General.

To set the stage for today's proceedings, Admiral RH Tahiliani, former Chief of Naval Staff and Governor of Sikkim has very kindly agreed to deliver the Keynote Address. I would like to place on record that the Admiral has been a pillar of strength to the USI and has always whole heartedly supported us in all our activities.

Admiral Tahiliani was India's Chief of Naval Staff from 1984-1987. After retirement, he served as the Governor of Sikkim from February 1990 to September 1994.

Admiral Tahiliani has been extremely active in charitable and social work after retirement. He is associated with Servants of the People Society, Lok Sevak Sangh and Transparency International India. Currently, he is the Chairman of Transparency International India. He is a member of the Central Vigilance Commission Advisory Council. He is also the Chairman of the Jasbhagti Charitable Society which works for the upliftment of the weaker sections of society.

Opening Remarks

❑ Mr Francois Stamm, HoRD of ICRC

Distinguished Participants, Ladies and Gentlemen,

The ICRC is honoured to co-organise this Seminar with the prestigious United Service Institution of India and it is my pleasure to welcome you to this event. I look forward to a day of intense and candid exchanges on an issue that is dear to the ICRC.

IHL, also known as the law of war or the law of armed conflict, is a part of international law, and seeks to mitigate the human suffering caused by armed conflicts. Essentially, it aims to humanise armed conflicts. The purpose of IHL is not to take war victims to heaven but to save them from hell. It seeks to reduce unnecessary human suffering during an armed conflict. It further seeks to mitigate the effects of war by limiting the choice of means and methods of conducting military operations, and by obliging the belligerents to spare persons who do not or who no longer participate in hostilities.

The present day rules of IHL are contained in a number of conventions dealing with matters ranging from the prohibition on the use of certain weapons, which cause indiscriminate damage and unnecessary suffering to those that deal with the protection of victims of armed conflict. Biological and Chemicals Weapons Conventions prohibit the use of such weapons. The Geneva Conventions and the additional protocols provide an extensive regime for the protection of persons not or no longer participating in direct hostilities. Ladies and gentlemen, the ICRC's view is that IHL shall remain relevant in 21st century conflict. We understand that different views, opinions exist, thus it is important to discuss this issue at length later today. It is true that the nature of conflict has changed over time. While 'traditional' inter-state conflicts have not disappeared, we are increasingly witnessing intra-state conflicts in different parts of the world that involve large number of different belligerents, both national and international. This has led to a number of new challenges in the implementation of IHL. Perhaps the greatest of these challenges is related to the struggle against terrorism, some thing that is important to explore in somewhat greater detail.

The increase in attention being paid to humanitarian law in recent times is the result mainly of the struggle against terrorism. The horrifying attacks of 11th September 2001 in New York and Washington and the response to them have raised question about the efficacy of IHL in dealing with contemporary forms of violence and in particular "terrorism". It has been asked whether IHL is actually capable of addressing terrorism ?

To answer this question we must clarify how different bodies of law relate to the term terrorism. Although a comprehensive definition at the international level does not exist, terrorist acts are well defined under domestic law and under existing international and regional conventions on terrorism and may, provided the requisite criteria are met, qualify as war crimes or as crimes against humanity. It is a basic principle of IHL that persons engaged in armed conflict must at all times distinguish between civilians and combatants and between civilian objects and military objectives. IHL also includes specific rules such as the prohibition against deliberate or direct attacks against civilian and civilian objects against indiscriminate attacks and use of "human shields". The taking of hostages is also prohibited. The IHL specifically prohibits "measures of terrorism" and "acts of terrorism" against persons in the power of a party to the conflict.

This important point should be understood. Unlike some other areas of international law, "terrorism" is well regulated under IHL, which explicitly prohibits acts committed against civilians and civilian objects in armed conflicts that would commonly be counted as "terrorist acts" if committed in peacetime.

In this context I would like to mention the growing and to us worrying tendency of States to label as "terrorists" all organised armed groups that oppose state authorities in non-international armed conflict. This trend to criminalise the enemy himself, and not just the specific acts he may carry out, goes against the need to differentiate between lawful acts of war in non-international armed conflicts and acts of terrorism. While acts of violence against military objectives in internal armed conflict remain subject to domestic criminal law, the tendency to also designate them as terrorist under international law risk undermining whatever little incentive armed groups have to respect IHL.

This leads me to my next observation on the legal definition of what some have called the "war against terrorism". The term has become very much part of daily parlance and makes the raising of this question necessary. Is this "war" an armed conflict in the legal sense as set out under humanitarian law? The answer is: No. In the struggle against terrorism the governments involve various legal, security and political measures such as gathering and sharing intelligence, freezing financial assets, establishing new security requirements or cooperating more closely with one another in the field of criminal prosecution. These means do not generally involve armed violence and certainly do not justify any reference to the law of war. However, the struggle against terrorism can sometimes be conducted by means of armed conflict. A case in point is the war in Afghanistan which began in 2001. In such a case the legal framework is as clear as any other armed conflict. IHL- is applicable.

However, the fact that the struggle against terrorism does sometimes take the form of armed conflict does not imply that the law regards all acts of terrorism carried out in various parts of the world, for instance the attacks in London, Madrid or Mumbai as belonging to the same armed conflict. It seems dubious to attribute the several acts to one identifiable party to armed conflict as understood under IHL or to claim that the level of violence in each instance is such as to qualify it to be regarded as armed conflict.

In conclusion, we know that each situation of organised violence must be examined in the specific context in which it takes place in order to establish on the basis of facts whether it qualifies legally as well. The laws were evolved to tackle situations of armed conflict both legally and practically. One should always remember that the provisions of humanitarian law on what constitutes lawful taking of life and on detention in armed conflict allow for more flexibility than the rules applicable in non-conflict situations governed by other bodies of law such as human rights law. In other words it is both unnecessary and dangerous to apply IHL to situations that do not amount to war. This is not always fully appreciated.

This being said I am not suggesting that there is no range for further clarification or development of IHL and the ICRC will remain closely involved in efforts to this effect.

I know that I have barely touched on the subject but I hope that we can explore some of these crucial issues during our discussions. Thank you for your kind attention and wish you all a wonderful and interactive learning and sharing experience. I would like again to thank the USI for the tremendous support they have provided us not only for this event but on other occasions and encouraging to make maximum use of this opportunity. Thank you.

Keynote Address

❑ Admiral RH Tahiliani, PVSM,AVSM (Retd) former CNS

I feel greatly honoured to have been invited to deliver this address on the subject of "The Continued Relevance of IHL in the 21st Century". This is a subject to which I had not applied my mind earlier. I must confess that I have learnt a thing or two while preparing for this morning's session. Having worn uniform for four decades one had come to accept or at least hope that the International conventions like the 1st, 2nd, 3rd and 4th Geneva Convention and the associated protocols were being implicitly followed by all parties in conflicts. In my 23 years of retirement and seeing that more and more non state actors are involved in conflicts and they are the ones who don't feel obliged to abide by any IHLs, I now believe that time has come for us to apply our minds to see whether we can formulate something with which we can persuade the non state actors also to abide by. I would like to compliment the Committee for the International Red Cross and the United Service Institution for organising this seminar this morning.

Although it may be a bit of diversion, many of the causes which generate conflicts by non state actors can be addressed by the states themselves. In our own country where tribal lands are taken from human beings where they have lived and earned their livelihood for centuries for the sake of economic development is one of the causes which generates conflicts. I have always believed that whereas economic development is a must for developing nations like ours, ways must be found to make those who are deprived of their lands and livelihood to become partners in the development process and wholeheartedly support the ventures. In some cases this has worked very successfully. This requires statesmanship which many of our today's politicians are probably not capable of. I was happy to read, however, that in the 35 districts which are critically affected by left wing extremism the government has decided to pump in an additional 45 to 50 crores each year to improve governance, roads, educational facilities, health centres, panchayats, etc., and to give tribals the right to use minor forest produce.

However, to come back to the main topic - Continued Relevance of the IHL in the 21st Century, there can be no two views about it. IHL's primary focus is to protect all those not involved in hostilities. The states have an obligation to teach its rules to their armed forces and the general public. States are also obliged to enact laws to punish the more serious violations of Geneva Conventions. The states must also pass laws protecting the Red Cross and the Red Crescent. At the international level tribunals must be created to punish crimes committed against IHL.

The basic rules of IHLs are :-

(a) Persons hors de combat and those who are not taking pact in hostilities shall be protected and treated humanely.

(b) It is forbidden to kill or injure an enemy who surrenders and who is hors de combat.

(c) The wounded and sick shall be cared for and protected by the party to the conflicts which have them in its power. The emblem of the 'Red Cross' and the "Red Crescent" shall be required to be respected as the sign of protection.

(d) Captured combatants and civilians must be protected against acts of violence and reprisals. They shall have the right to correspond with their families and to receive relief.

(e) No one shall be subjected to torture, corporal, cruel or degrading punishment.

(f) Parties to a conflict and members of their armed forces do not have an unlimited choice of methods and means of warfare.

(g) Parties to a conflict shall at al times distinguish between civilian population and combatants. Attacks shall be directed solely against military objectives.

Examples, well known of such rules include the prohibition on attacking doctors or ambulances displaying a Red Cross. It is also prohibited to fire at a person or a vehicle with a 'white flag' since that being considered the flag of truce indicates an intent to surrender or a desire to communicate. In either case, the persons protected by the Red Cross or the white flag are expected to maintain neutrality and they may not engage in war like acts themselves. In fact, engaging in war activities under a 'white flag' or a Red Cross is itself a violation of the laws of war.

In recent years IHL has come to the forefront of public interest and debate because some voices have challenged the relevance of these to contemporary conflicts suggesting that it is ill-equipped to deal with the threats posed to states when confronting non-state armed groups. The decades-long conflict between Sri

Lankan government forces and the LTTE, the protracted 10-year struggle between the Nepalese Government forces and the Maoists and the ongoing insurgency in Afghanistan, are a few examples.

While the IHL continues to be relevant in the 21st Century, and I can't see how it can ever be not relevant even in subsequent centuries. The United Nations has crafted the following instruments which enforce the aims and objectives of IHL. These are :-

(a) Standard Minimum Rules for the Treatment of Prisoners in 1957.

(b) Declaration Against Torture and other Cruel, Inhuman or degrading Treatment or Punishment, 1975.

(c) Code of Conduct for Law Enforcement Officials, 1979.

(d) Safeguards Guaranteeing Protection of the Rights of Those Facing The Death Penalty, 1984.

(e) Basic Principles on the Independence of the Judiciary, 1985.

(f) Model Agreement to the Transfer of Foreign Prisoners and Recommendations on the Treatment of Foreign Prisoners 1985.

(g) Principles of Justice for Victims of Crime and the Abuse of Power in 1985.

(h) Standard Minimum Rules for the Non Custodial Measures.

(j) Basic Principles On The Use Of Force And Firearms By Law Enforcement Officials.

(k) Model Treaty on Extradition, Model Treaty on Mutual Assistance in Criminal Matters.

(l) Model Treaty on the Transfer of Proceedings In Criminal Cases.

(m) Resolution on Measures Against International Terrorism.

The underlying theme of all these conventions and efforts by the UN is protection of human rights of all and treatment of the enemy with decency. This is the core theme that has come to stay and that determines the foreign policy as well as collaborations of various countries.

As and when the problems arise the UN is sure to alert all the nations to take suitable action. These instruments have already affected legal frameworks in the form of legal enactments. I am happy to report that in our Country in the post-1971 war as has been mentioned, all the prisoners who were taken from our adversary were treated humanely and in due process returned to their mother country. I would wish this seminar great success because of its importance to humanity. Humanity will continue to endeavour to frame all these laws and protocols in order to ensure that the long term goal of all on this planet live in peace and harmony. Hopefully, it will come about one day, although it may not come about in my lifetime. Thank you for inviting me, good luck, God bless you.

Session – I

International Humanitarian Law and Laws of Armed Conflict with regard to 21st Century Conflicts – The ICRC Experience in Sri Lanka

Chairman	-	Lt Gen AS Kalkat,SYSM, PVSM,AVSM,VSM (Retd)
Speaker	-	Mr Paul Castella, HoD ICRC Colombo

Chairman's Remarks

❑ Lieutenant General AS Kalkat, SYSM,PVSM,AVSM,VSM (Retd)

I have been invited to chair this Session because the topic includes 'The ICRC Experience in Sri Lanka' and I had it in plenty before the ICRC got into the act. I hope the representation by Mr Paul Castella, HoD, ICRC, Colombo, will bring out many points, because there are certain questions being asked. This is an appropriate occasion for the participants to air their views and also to get certain issues clarified.

Before the speaker takes on the subject, please note that the IPKF went there long before the ICRC got into the act. This is not to say that the ICRC office was not present in Colombo - but they were not in the conflict area. When the IPKF arrived in 1987, there were far too many casualties, much more than what the military operations had anticipated. The scaling of the medical support was inadequate to meet the needs. We also found that we had inadequate medical facilities not only to treat our own soldiers and of course the prisoners that we captured, as also the civilian population which either got involved in collateral damage or were otherwise already in need of medical aid.

Because there were no organisations forthcoming in Sri Lanka, international or national, a request was sent to our Prime Minister in Delhi. An Indian Red Cross team was sent from India and it began to operate there. Obviously, since the Indian Red Cross was a part of the ICRC, it got involved in Sri Lanka also. However, I am not aware whether ICRC was actively involved with them at that time. I may also mention that it was the first casualty the Indian Red Cross suffered in Sri Lanka. The driver of an ambulance was killed by terrorists. I hope it is in the records of ICRC, if not, they might like to add it.

While speaking on this occasion I think it is appropriate that Admiral Tahiliani, one of the founders of the Indian Peace Keeping Force (IPKF), gave the Keynote address today. He is not only the founder of the IPKF, but it was his vision that perceived the joint force going in. He took a lot of interest, even to the extent of designing the flag of the IPKF, which is not commonly known. So, if there are any questions on the concept or the start of the IPKF operations in Sri Lanka, apart from me, (I am emboldened by the fact) that I have my mentor here who would be able to answer where I cannot.

I now invite Mr Paul Castella, Head of the Delegation of ICRC in Colombo, to speak on 'The ICRC Experience on the Conflict in Sri Lanka'. He has been there from 2008. The conflict started long before that. But I am sure he has sufficient background knowledge and expertise available in the organisation there, to be able to answer all the questions. He is eminently qualified because he has been the Head of Delegation at many places - in Russia and in Kabul, Afghanistan (1993-94). Those were the years before the global war on terror started but, nevertheless, IHLs were still being violated. With that I request Mr Paul Castella to take over.

Session I : Paper

❑ Mr Paul Castella, HoD, ICRC Colombo

Admiral Tahliani, General PK Singh and distinguished participants. Thank you very much for allowing me to speak in front of you today. Before starting the presentation, I would like to mention that this is the second time I am having the privilege of talking in New Delhi about ICRC experiences in Sri Lanka. However, for one reason or the other, I always feel like a first year student writing an examination, when I do so; and with General Kalkat's introductory remarks, I feel even more nervous than usual because I know that many of you have better knowledge and personal experience about this conflict. Therefore, I apologise at the outset, if I miss out something. I am also not sure whether I will be able to answer all your questions; even then, I will try to do my best.

What I will present to you is mainly my experiences during the last stages of the conflict because that is when I was present. Of course, I would try to answer more questions, if you have any. I will use the experience gained during these last stages of the conflict to illustrate what International Humanitarian Law (IHL) is or could be in a modern conflict. It would not be, of course, about reporting on how well or not the two parties respected IHL. The purpose of my speech is, as you will see in the second part, in line with the tasks given by ICRC Statutes - (which are endorsed by the States parties to the Geneva Conventions). It will cover what we have done in Sri Lanka and elsewhere in the world through bilateral and comprehensive dialogue. I will not touch upon the issues that are still under discussion with responsible authorities in Sri Lanka or elsewhere in the world. I will just talk about the situation, as seen and experienced by me in Sri Lanka, and I hope you will understand that.

I will begin by briefly touching upon the law, with short references just to illustrate precisely how IHL can be applied. As you know, IHL application in Sri Lanka is limited to the Common Article 3 and to customary IHL because Sri Lanka, as India, is not a party to Additional Protocol 2. Should or would Sri Lanka have become a party to Additional Protocol 2, we at the ICRC would have, of course, suggested that this should have been applied, which is why I am mentioning it in this presentation, even though legally speaking this is not applicable.

I will go through three stages in my presentation, the first one is : *How IHL can be applied in reality in the Combat Zone and heat of the battlefield ? The second will be more about the areas surrounding the Combat Zone, i.e. after the fighting had stopped, where does the IHL apply and lastly, of course, would be the conclusions.*

Firstly, a short reference to IHL in the Combat Zone. I would like to mention just two points, because Admiral Tahiliani has already explained very well the concept of law and the issues about distinction and proportionality in using force. The first point is about '*prohibition of relief actions to be undertaken'.* A very important aspect considering that, as you know very well, in Sri Lanka part of the Sri Lankan population was living under the control or authority of another party, not the Government; so how to handle that aspect ? I think that was an interesting challenge. In addition all the authorities are part of customary IHL. Another point that is interesting is the '*protection of safe areas'.* This was an interesting concept that was used, or attempted to be used, in Sri Lanka. It would be useful to discuss this a little later.

What was interesting in the last stages of the conflict, concerning the application of IHL, is based on maps that I have taken from the Ministry of Defence website. The big challenge facing the Sri Lankan security forces as they were advancing was not in the areas that they had gained control of initially; but it was much more serious in the last stages of the conflict. After gaining control of the areas in the initial stages, the issue of respect of IHL was not as serious as it was during the last part. Why? It is because in the beginning, the distinction between who was fighting and who was not directly involved in hostilities, was not so difficult to make. There were issues, of course, but it was clear where the fighting was taking place. The frontline was quite mobile and the population managed to escape largely the effects of the fighting. However, in the last part it was very different; because, there the armed forces were facing a big challenge. On the one hand, the population was being trapped and very few could leave this area because of various reasons, while on the other, the ability to make a distinction between those fighting and others who were not taking part in direct hostilities, was much more difficult. That was of course Part I. Part II was in an area that was shrinking and, therefore, the military and security forces could use more troops to fight the last stages of the war in that smaller area. Therefore, this became a dilemma; as, now they had more troops and more firepower. However, there was also a greater difficulty in applying IHL as making a precise distinction (between combatant and non-combatant) had become more difficult. Therefore, the Sri Lanka forces faced a huge challenge.

Now, I will present a few examples of how we could overcome these challenges in order to have IHL respected, as Admiral Tahiliani has just explained? The first, of a few examples, is the '*Concept of Safe Areas*'. The use of a safe area was attempted in Sri Lanka, like elsewhere, to precisely allow the '*Rule of Distinction' to apply.* Those not taking part in the fighting could go to the safe areas, allowing the adversary to distinguish between combatants and non-combatants and to fight against only those outside of the safe area. This is the principle of the safe area. The two safe areas that were declared by the Government simultaneously were established consecutively. The first one was set-up with the hope that the population would later go north or west towards Killinochi. This information was gained through our contacts in the military. Later, the nature of fighting changed the situation because the population eventually went east rather than going north and that is why a decision was made to set-up a second safety zone along the seacoast, at the shore line. So, these were the two attempts.

I will say just a few more words about the safe areas. Safe areas are of course a very interesting and possibly useful concept to apply IHL, but they are very difficult to maintain and a very sensitive issue. Why? It is difficult because, in order for a safe area to work, you must have mutual agreement between both parties otherwise it does not work. That is the first point. The second point is about exercising control in safe areas or the rules of the game applying to safe areas; meaning that inside the safe areas should be only people that are not taking part in the hostilities and those taking part should remain outside of them. So, how to control that? I think this is a big challenge and it was very difficult in Sri Lanka to exercise control. We were asked to have a look at this aspect; but of course, we simply had to decline this proposal because there is no way that we could ever enforce the rules of the game. Those who followed Sri Lankan operations know that the LTTE was responsible for a safe area in the Jaffna peninsula. This was around the main hospital in Jaffna and it worked very well. It was, however, a different situation in the heat of the battle in the last stages of the combat. It was a sensitive situation. It was very attractive for people who were not taking direct part in hostilities to go to these areas because they would feel safe. However, how could you guarantee that they would be safe there, when you could not control those who were fighting from entering the area?. So, safe areas would give the impression to the population that they would have protection under IHL and would be safe. This is, however, not always the case and of course all of us have in mind the terrible tragic example of the Balkans, where the population was eventually precisely targeted. So, the safe area is a very interesting tool, but I think it is a very difficult and sensitive one to maintain. This is the first example that I wanted to share with you.

The second example is related to the start of the battle for the town of Killinochi where the ICRC offices were located. What I want to bring out is that in a situation where combat operations take place, the '*rule of 'distinction'* is of course important, but how to apply it is one of the challenges. One way is to give to the other party the precise GPS coordinates of the objectives that are protected under IHL, to ensure that their location is well known to the other party and so they can be safe and not targeted by accident or even otherwise. The big problem in Sri Lanka, during the last stages of the conflict, was that the frontline was moving quite rapidly. Sometimes overnight, the progress was a few kilometres and sometimes it was as much as 10 kilometres. Therefore, it was very difficult for the other party to know where these protected objectives were. Hospitals were moved from one place to another, with the possibility of the new location being either a school or a tent, which would of course be not known to the other party and, therefore, could be targeted. During the last stages of the conflict, we tried to ensure, as much as possible, that both parties would know where these protected objectives were. The lists of GPS coordinates about our offices were also handed over to both parties for our own safety and protection, as was information about the place where hospitals were. Therefore, it was a continuous fight to obtain these GPS coordinates and transmit them to the military, e.g. to the artillery, air force and so on, so that they would know where these protected objectives were. This was really a race against time. Nevertheless, I think this is a very important aspect to keep in mind, remembering that it was a very difficult one, and hopefully it served some purpose.

The third illustration of how to implement IHL is, for example, the known '*cross line*.' During the ceasefire in 2002, there were three crossing lines officially opened to allow the movement of people and goods across the lines e.g. the Omentai crossing point. These crossing points were essential to allow the movement of goods. We had hundreds of thousands of people in the areas that needed food and healthcare. So, these crossing lines were kept open officially under ICRC authority in order to ensure safe movement. However, for both warring parties, this was a '*weak point*' because it was a door that remained open to either party; both used them either to infiltrate, or to attack, and so on. Therefore, we very often had to discuss incidents but also attempt to restore trust between the parties about these crossing lines to ensure that people could continue to cross. Each of these locations was negotiated with the two parties to ensure that the other side knew the locations of the barriers so that their positioning was not seen as an attempt to prepare for an attack or something like that. We were responsible to ensure that this trust was maintained through a regular flow of information. Both sides obviously did the security checks. Traffic was controlled to ensure that security was being maintained. It was a very difficult job for the security personnel in charge of these points. Keeping them open, when there is fighting, is a very difficult task. We had to close the crossing line more than once because of shelling in the area. Of course, both parties became nervous and the traffic was stopped. Patients that needed to be evacuated were stranded and it was hard to handle these issues. A very interesting mechanism was set-up during the last stages of the conflict. It was even more difficult to keep the door open while the frontline was changing. We had many discussions every day with both parties on how to ensure that this happened. This was a difficult challenge because the roads could not be used due to military operations and we had to then resort to the sea route.

We had two agreements with the Government forces and the LTTE. On the ground, we had the declared '*safe area*' that would allow patients to be collected, moved to the shore, embarked on the ships (on fishing boats, actually) and then taken out to sea. We had another agreement that was in respect to a much larger area where they agreed that there would be no military craft. Our main patient evacuation ship was berthed around this area. We had an agreement about the size of this safe area and we gave the GPS coordinates to both parties to ensure that there was no problem. This was a failure, of course. In practice every day, you had to fight for it *(the safe area)* because the Sri Lankan Navy, which was further out in the deep sea, was sealing off the coast to ensure there would be no supply to and no escape for the LTTE. On the other side, the LTTE was also trying hard to keep the Sri Lankan Navy out to sea, as far as possible. So, we were in between; and of course, we had Sea Tigers boats in the area. We had to ask them to move. Application of IHL is definitely not easy. Nevertheless, up to the last stage, until I think five days before the end of the war, we could maintain this evacuation route open, which was fantastic and some goods could still be brought in. It was a very enlightening experience on how IHL could be applied even in the heat of the conflict.

Now, I would move away from the conflict zone to give you some examples of how IHL was also applicable further away, which again had some legal aspects. The first one is about the movement of population - the Sinhala population. I will talk here about displacement. Displacement is something that happens in almost every conflict, be it small or extensive, and it is most of the time unavoidable. IHL regulates the responsibility in cases of forced displacement but also in cases of returning population, because there is also a '*right for return in safety*'. I will give some hints on these aspects. Displacement of the population was a huge challenge facing the authorities. More than 200,000 people left the conflict zone and came into what was called Government-controlled territory. What to do with this population? The challenge for the Government was two-fold. First was security. Of course, insurgent sympathisers made up part of this population, so there was the right and duty of the Government forces to ensure that they could screen these persons according to their mandate. Secondly, a decision was made, probably because of security, to establish new camps and not to locate or settle these persons in the camps that existed previously in schools and churches or any other places. This was a very difficult decision because these camps were taken away from the forest so everything had to be started from scratch. There was absolutely nothing, no drinking water and it was raining as well. In the end, the camps were established in an area that was initially forest and then eventually people were moved into these camps. It was a huge challenge for the authorities.

What is very important when you look at IHL being applied is: How to plan ahead, how to work with others; not just the military or the security forces; but also with senior administration, humanitarian and faith based organisations who have also some ability to help. When you face such a challenge I think IHL pushes you to move really further ahead and widen the scope.

The big challenge was, of course, that the camps were set-up along the road, which was quite logical, but the main issue was the water supply. The Government and the concerned authorities were thinking of pumping water from existing water reservoirs. In the northern part of the country, they have many of these water reservoirs. However, if they did this, then they would not have enough water for rice cultivation. So, they had to make decisions that were sometimes very harmful for the local population, a big dilemma. I wanted to mention that this issue of displacement of population is something that needs to be planned ahead. Establishing partnerships would also be useful.

Here, besides the needs of the displaced population; you also had to see the issue of the wounded and the sick; as amongst the 200,000 displaced people, many were wounded and even more were sick. What to do with them? How to put health structures in place to face the sudden increase in needs? The other category of population that we had to look out for, were of course the '*detainees*'. According to official figures, there were some 8000 or so LTTE suspects detained. There was also a sudden increase of the prison population. What to do with them was a dilemma?

The ICRC supported the local authorities on another very simple aspect, the effort and effect of which should not be underestimated, and that is the issue of '*dead bodies' management*'. Simply the authorities were not able to face this huge challenge and we helped them to build the capacity for keeping the dead bodies until they were identified and then taken care of according to their religion. This is what happens on the ground. I will not go much more into detail because what I am talking about is happening now so it is a bit early to learn lessons from it.

In the end, I want to make mention of three other big challenges. One is the '*resettlement*' of displaced persons. It is a huge challenge nowadays because you cannot simply return them to a place that is not prepared for them; and the main issue here, as we know, is 'land mines'. According to the authorities, they would not have an overall idea of the situation regarding the areas that are contaminated or not before the end of the year. Only later will they have the statistics to allow for demining or the decontamination to take place. It has started already but this according to specialists is probably an endeavour that would take years. This is again, something to plan ahead as there are a lot of financial issues involved and all these activities cost money. Another challenge is '*war victims*'. Many people were wounded, like in every war, leaving behind many physically as well as mentally disabled people. I am not talking here only about civilians but about military personnel as well, and this is again a sad challenge for the Country as a whole to face. The last point, as I mentioned before, is the '*handling of some 8000-suspected LTTE militants*'. What to do with them? It is not only caring for them i.e. the providing of shelter, food, hygiene, healthcare and so on; but what to actually do with them is a big issue which, having talked to the senior-most General, is a big problem. He had to increase his team in order to handle these cases. So, when you look at IHL and what the Law says, and if you look at to the consequences of the implementation of the Law, you see that it is very broad in scope and often long lasting. These are the initial lessons that we learnt from this conflict.

Conclusion

In accordance with the discussions I had with people on the ground, I have concluded that IHL is not just a legal tool. I think it is a tool for commanders at different levels to think of the challenges of tomorrow and to plan. This is because the people, who have gone through wars, drafted IHL. *What to do with prisoners, what to do with the wounded and what to do with civilians that are displaced and how they can be returned*? According to what I discussed with commanders, they see IHL as a kind of checklist to start working on. Secondly, in non-international armed conflicts, the legal obligations are often less when compared to international armed conflicts. Non-international armed conflicts deal with a country's own citizens. Sometimes it can be quite strange to see that less legal obligations apply under IHL when you deal with your own citizens compared to when you deal with foreigners. That is why military commanders have told me many times recently that they now have to be humanitarian actors because they feel that they have a role to play. They have to care for the needs of the population, simply because their duty to restore control over the territory is over, and now see that they have a new role to play in the recovery phase. We see their role as being a partner to ICRC, and other humanitarian organisations. That is why I am writing here that we see their role going forward far greater than just what the law says. Their responsibility is more. That is an interesting thought that I wanted to share and to discuss with you.

Thank you very much.

Session I - Discussion (Q & A)

Issues Raised

(a) Can you give us the quantum of the forces deployed by the ICRC in Sri Lanka in terms of the personnel, ambulances, vehicles and the quantum of medicines that were provided ?

(b) Did you interact with the United Nations High Commission for Refugees (UNHCR) or did Sri Lankan government do so ?

(c) What was the ICRC's role vis-à-vis the UNHCR ? Did you coordinate between the concerned parties ?

(d) Did you involve yourselves at any stage in any political dialogue or discussions with the LTTE and others ?

Responses

(a) Firstly, about the resources in Sri Lanka, it is difficult to quantify them as a whole. By the end of the war, ICRC had deployed approximately 650 staff personnel – today, the number is about half of that because the need is less. ICRC policy about resources in general is that it invests in the resources that are required. But, ICRC of course, prefers to supplement the resources existing in the country, to play a supporting role. Whenever necessary, ICRC substitutes its resources, but that was not the case in Sri Lanka, which is a very resourceful country in many aspects. As far as the quantum of ambulances, medicines and hospitals etc, it varied according to the need at different times. During operations in the combat zone ICRC had combos, which included trucks which would carry items like tents, water and food etc. When the war ended the ICRC moved to sea operations on a ship to allow the relatives of patients to unite with them. In that way ICRC varies its efforts according to the needs. For example, at the height of the conflict ICRC provided four or five ambulances in the conflict zone, where the requirement was acute and urgent.

(b) On interaction with the UN and UNHCR authorities, ICRC's role is complementary to other humanitarian organisations. The interaction and coordination with others is as much as is required to meet the assessed needs. ICRC's main counterpart in such matters is of course the government authority, and it does useful work in tandem with them. For example, the ICRC coordinated with UNHCR, when the persons came out of the conflict zone – the UNHCR provided one type of assistance and we provided the another.

(c) ICRC is a humanitarian organisation, therefore, it does not engage in political discussions. We did, however, have discussions with the LTTE to carry out our humanitarian mandate and that was done at the level of the political wing of the LTTE. At the early stages, ICRC's highest contact for dealing with political aspects was with Mr Premadasan – being the only international organisation allowed in the conflict zone. ICRC also carried messages on behalf of the government or the LTTE on to the other side. ICRC has been working as a neutral intermediary, whenever asked. In Sri Lanka, sometimes confidential dialogues did take place between the authorities and on behalf of the LTTE, mainly on humanitarian considerations.

Issue Raised

Was it with the concurrence of the Sri Lankan government or the ICRC did it independently?

Response

In carrying out humanitarian mandate the ICRC bases its actions on the statutes that are issued based on the Geneva Conventions; and of course in full agreement with the government authorities present there. In Sri Lanka, ICRC's mandate was specifically requested by the government, and it did, what it was requested to do. There is an important point to note - ICRC's main counterparts are the other governments because they are a party to the Geneva Conventions.

Issue Raised

Is there a preventive detention law for rehabilitation of 8000 suspected LTTE cadres, applicable in Sri Lanka ?

Responses

(a) The Sri Lankan government has a plan of rehabilitation for detained LTTE personnel. Since it has not been spelt out in its entirety, this question cannot be answered fully. Under the authority of the Ministry of Disaster Management and Human Rights, which does not exist any more, an interesting plan called the '*National Plan for the Social Reintegration of ex-LTTE Combatants*' was worked out by their counterparts in various Ministries. This plan exists, but whether different rehabilitation aspects as per the plan are online, can be confirmed by the Sri Lankan government only.

(b) In Sri Lanka Preventive Detention Laws are still promulgated today, on a monthly basis. These Laws allow the arrest and detention of a number of persons in accordance with its provisions. They also have a 'Terrorism Prevention Act', which is a second set of laws that allow the arrest and detention of people. So, actually they have two sets of laws that exist.

Issue Raised

What has been the ICRC role in demining operations ?

Response

Initially, the ICRC did not have a role in demining. However, the ICRC has decided to acquire some skills in this aspect – by establishing partnership with demining organisations. ICRC does not have an inherent capacity in demining. However, wherever a need is felt for deploying such competencies on partnership basis, the ICRC response is strictly limited to 'demining', when it is affecting the livelihood of the population. The ICRC does not undertake large scale demining operations.

Issue Raised

The Sri Lankan government after defeating the LTTE, is now discussing the political settlement. When does the ICRC envisage that its role and job in Sri Lanka would be over or what would be the best time for it to go back to Geneva or any other place?

Response

The ICRC acts on humanitarian considerations. Therefore, it does not base its action on the political situation. It does so on the existence of needs and on application of law. In Sri Lanka, as everyone knows, the need continues to exist; large populations have still not completely returned home. Large number of people are still detained and there are many wounded in hospitals who need help. The IHL continues to offer protection to certain categories of detainees during the conflict. ICRC would, therefore, continue to have its work cut out, until the situation becomes normal. The presence and strength of ICRC is reviewed and reduced constantly. Due to limited resources, ICRC does not aim to stay in a country for long, unless it is needed there. It would continue to stay in Sri Lanka as long as it is needed and also if the government authorities share ICRC views on such needs. Of course, as the needs decrease, the plan is to continue to reduce its deployment and strength of personnel.

Issue Raised

What is the ICRC's relationship with the Sri Lankan Government ? Does their presence in the conflict zone hamper the security of government plans and operations?

Response

The Sri Lankan government allowed the ICRC to remain in the conflict zone. It is the only international humanitarian organisation which has established a lot of trust with the government. Although, the government was concerned about the safety of ICRC personnel and being harmed by the LTTE; but they accepted the challenge and allowed them to continue working there. Implementation of IHL sometimes creates difficulties and this aspect merits serious consideration for establishing mutual trust between the affected parties.

Issues Raised

(a) In the global context, at what stage of a conflict does the ICRC get sucked in? Is it at the instance of the government or the other parties ? How are their concerns addressed ?

(b) In case of under developed countries, the ICRC do not have adequate resources in terms of manpower, monitoring, logistics, the ability to go to every part because they do not have aviation assets. In such situations at what stage does the ICRC get involved with the UN on planning and deciding areas, to form part of their peacekeeping and social development programmes ?

Response

(a) The ICRC starts its operations after due discussions with the governments because they are the main counterparts to facilitate their working in the areas of conflict. Of course, the ICRC firstly, starts such discussions based on their own independent assessment of needs. This right was given to the ICRC under the Statute which is acknowledged by the governments and parties to the Geneva Conventions. The ICRC has the right to propose and then, the governments being sovereign have a right to refuse, decline or to accept.

(b) Due to lack of resources the ICRC are facing situations where their response is limited and they contribute by answering part of the problems only. Very often humanitarian problems have deeply anchored roots in the peculiar socio-economic system of a country. Much of the efforts then depends on help from other donors – who act out of compassion on humanitarian grounds. ICRC, however, endeavours to do its best with the resources at their disposal.

(c) ICRC is not part of the UN system. It is a part of the International Red Cross movement and, therefore, not an integral part of the UN planning. However, ICRC does coordinate with the UN systems on certain aspects. But, it is separate and independent from the UN system and is not involved in planning with them.

Issue Raised

According to the LTTE, the ICRC has not done enough for them. What is the ICRC response to such complaints ?

Response

The ICRC tries to do its best depending on the goodwill of the two parties or more than two parties involved in the conflict. If one of the party is not interested it is very difficult to go ahead because the ICRC works in agreement with the parties. The ICRC does not have any armed protection, except in one or two areas because of criminality. The protection of ICRC personnel is based on the 'agreement' and 'trust' with all the parties. Sometimes in the perception of one or the other party the ICRC may not have done enough, but whenever the ICRC becomes aware of a problem, it always to tries do its best.

Issue Raised

During the Sri Lanka conflict, were there any lapses detected, which would amount to breaches of conventions and additional protocols ? What corrective measures have been initiated with regard to the implementation and enforcement of the IHL?

Response

IHL is not a rule that will be applied always, everywhere and at all times. There are always breaches, the way traffic laws are violated all over the world. However, the ICRC role with regards to breaches is to report these breaches , to the concerned authorities only, for initiating appropriate action. ICRC is not an adjudicatory organisation, but it aims to support the authorities who have accepted to abide by the IHL. Accordingly, in Sri Lanka or elsewhere the ICRC is helpful in circulating information to the concerned systems to facilitate redressal of violations wherever they happen. In this regard, ICRC maintains strict confidentiality but sometimes the other parties do not. ICRC has a very clean record in Sri Lanka on this account.

Closing Remarks by the Chairman

It only remains for me to thank Mr Paul Castella for a very frank and a very comprehensive presentation. Obviously, in a short time given to him he could not have told you everything. However, the fact is that he has brought out the main architecture of the ICRC involvement and experience in the Sri Lankan conflict, both in his presentation and in answering some thought provoking questions.

However, there is always a question : When should the ICRC go away or when should its role stop ? To this, the answer is, that even though the IHL is not invoked in certain situations; but the 'human rights' law shall always be applicable everywhere in the civilised world and that has the sanction of the United Nations Charter. Thank you.

Session II

Human Rights and the Indian Armed Forces

Chairman	-	Lt Gen Vijay Oberoi, PVSM,AVSM,VSM (Retd)
Speakers	-	Maj Gen Nilendra Kumar, AVSM,VSM (Retd)
	-	Lt Gen P C Katoch,PVSM,UYSM, AVSM,SC (Retd)

Chairman's Opening Remarks

❑ Lieutenant General Vijay Oberoi, PVSM,AVSM, VSM (Retd), former VCOAS

General PK Singh, Mr Stamm, distinguished guests, ladies and gentlemen. Firstly, I am very happy to have been invited to chair this session on the subject '*Human Rights and the Indian Armed Forces*'. The topic is of great relevance today when a large component of the Indian Army is deployed and is conducting CI and CT operations. I have, as my fellow panelists, two experts who can articulate on the subject both from their practical experience and through their academic pursuits.

By way of introducing the subject, I will say a few words. There is a difference between International Humanitarian Law (IHL) and Human Rights (HR). IHL deals essentially with the laws of war and armed conflicts. On the other hand HR also extend to the civilian world i.e. to everybody in the civilian domain whether they are in the conflict zone or not. The convergence of these two subjects is a recent phenomenon. In Additional Protocol No 2 of 1977, an attempt has been made to cover all kinds of conflicts i.e. international as well as non-international. By non-international, we mean non-state actors that are involved in the fighting. However, non-state actors do not figure in the prevalent humanitarian regimes, simply because they are not organised entities - whose members can be held responsible for the violations. These individuals and organisations do not respect any laws and conventions. They bring to bear overwhelming brutality and ruthlessness in their actions while pursuing their goals. They kill and maim security forces personnel as well as innocent civilians with equal ferocity.

The nuances of HR are not new for the Indian Armed Forces. I am sure the panelists will amplify the points which I am making, as they have been engaged in fighting with the militants, terrorists and insurgents in different formats for almost half a century. While most were and are Indian nationals, we have also dealt with insurgents from other countries e.g. the LTTE in Sri Lanka and a variety of foreign nationals in the ongoing insurgency in J&K. I am specially making this point because the way the Indian army deals with insurgency and terrorism is different from what the other armies do. I want to emphasise that we have done so both for domestic as well as non-domestic terrorists. This is a point of great relevance, which we must remember.

With this brief introduction gentlemen, we will start Session-II by introducing our panelists. The first speaker is Major General Nilendra Kumar. He is an expert in military law besides other facets of law. While in service, he dealt with all aspects of 'Human Rights', especially those that are relevant to the Army. He will present his views on the subject '*Human Rights and the Indian Armed Forces*'. Our second speaker, Lieutenant General Prakash Chand Katoch, from the Parachute Regiment, is a highly decorated officer with wide experience in all types of terrain and warfare, including fighting insurgents of the LTTE in Sri Lanka while serving with the unit of the Special Forces. He would be presenting his views on the subject *"International Humanitarian Law – a Combat Leader's View"*. I would now request the first speaker to take the floor.

Session II – First Paper

❑ Major General Nilendra Kumar, AVSM, VSM* (Retd)

The term Human Rights was first introduced in the American Declaration of Independence in 1776 and found place in the United States Bill of Rights. Human Rights have been defined as those basic inalienable and fundamental rights as well as freedoms which every citizen enjoys irrespective of the country that he belongs to. Human Rights are universal and belong to everyone, rich or poor, male or female. Such rights may be violated but they can never be taken away. However, there is no consensus as to the precise nature of what in particular should or should not be regarded as Human Rights. The abstract concept of Human Rights has been a subject of considerable discussion and criticism.

These rights are often grouped in three categories vis-à-vis first generation, second generation and third generation rights. First generation rights are the basic Human Rights necessary for physical existence and spiritual needs of human body. These would include right to live and right to worship. Second generation rights are those that relate to political, educational and commercial sphere. The third generation rights are also called inter generation rights which pertain to environment or heritage etc.

A discussion on Human Rights in the context of Armed Forces raises certain political, legal and humanitarian issues giving rise to intense debate. It is often pointed out that the soldiers, though perceived as defenders of the national security, have at times indulged in violation of Human Rights, and further the civil administration affords them unjustified protection. These rights stand abused and disregarded. On the other hand, it is argued that a section of the media and interested elements often criticize them with malafide intent.

An objective scrutiny of the role of the Armed Forces requires suitable appraisal of the relevant articles of Constitution of India provision besides the provisions of Army Act, 1950. The Armed Forces (Special Powers) Act, 1958 and The Protection of Human Rights Act, 1993.

Human Rights in the Indian context are akin to fundamental rights included in Part-III of the Constitution of India. The latter does not use the term Human Rights but has enumerated a number of 'Fundamental Rights'. The two terms could be viewed as synonymous. Each of these fundamental rights[1] is available to all citizens and in some cases to the non citizen also. Thus, every citizen can claim a number of Fundamental Rights. But are these available in equal measure and to the same extent to the soldiers?

It would be pertinent to note that by virtue of Article 33[2] of the Constitution, the Parliament stands empowered to restrict or abrogate any or all of the fundamental rights in their application to Armed Forces personnel. However, such a restriction or curtailment may only be effected for fulfilling two fold objective of better performance of their duty and for maintenance of proper discipline. Thus it is the specific mandate of Article 33 which sanctifies denial of freedom of speech or withholding the Armed Forces personnel from forming any union or to join a trade union etc. This aspect is relevant to answer the off-repeated query whether the military personnel enjoy Human Rights or is it only a notion applicable to the militants. On the other spectrum of the discussion is the case of those persons whose Human Rights may be alleged to have been denied by the Armed Forces personnel. Is there any law to deal with their grievances? Are they entitled to any meaningful protection and in case found to be actually aggrieved liable to any compensation? What is the statutory mechanism to examine their complaints?

The next relevant provision in this regard is the Protection of Human Rights Act, 1993[3]. The preamble of the statute records that it has been enacted for better protection of Human Rights and for matters connected therewith.

Protection of Human Rights Act provided for setting up of a National Human Rights Commission (NHRC), State Human Rights Commissions and for enforcement of Human Rights regime by Human Rights Force. NHRC has been invested with powers to undertake investigations in situations involving violation of Human Rights[4]. The major functions of NHRC are to enquire violations of Human Rights. Such an enquiry[5] can be triggered on receipt of a petition or suo-moto. NHRC can intervene in any proceedings concerning denial or suppression of Human Rights[6]. It has been authorised to visit a jail or other institution with a view to examine efficacy of safeguards provided under the Constitution[7]. It is also empowered to study treaties and other international instruments and make recommendations to see best practices in an international perspective. However, a different procedure has been indicated with regard to allegations about its authority to examine adherence to Human Rights norms by the Armed Forces personnel[8]. Relevant provisions in this regard lay down that while dealing with complaints of violation of Human Rights by members of Armed forces, the commission shall either on its motion or on receipt of petition, seek a report from the Central Government.

After receipt of the report, the Commission may

(a) Either decide not to proceed with the complaint.

(b) Or, may make its recommendation to the Government.

The Central Government shall inform the Commission of the action taken on the recommendations.

One of the major criticism of the provision of the Protection of Human Rights Act is its inability to investigate reports of allegations of Human Rights violations by the men in uniform. The reasons for such a scheme treating Armed Forces personnel on a different footing is not hard to understand. It is because the military law is a self contained code which is equipped with an adequate mechanism for investigation of offences by providing for a system to undertake enquiries by courts or boards of enquiry[9]. Therefore, to rule out any scope for duplicity or contradiction, an entry to NHRC to undertake investigation into role of military personnel has been shut down and provision of a probe by Courts of enquiry have been retained. It is often lost sight of that NHRC has been barred to examine violation of Human Rights *by* members of the Armed Forces and not *of* (emphasis supplied) them. However, there is no embargo on NHRC taking up for examination any allegation involving violation of Human Rights of Armed Forces personnel, or say a visit to any military prison or detention centre where a person in uniform may have been kept in illegal or improper custody.

Other major aspects connecting Human Rights and Armed Forces personnel is the issue pertaining to certain significant authority given to the military men under Armed Forces (Special Powers) Act, 1958 (in short AFSPA). This Act was designed to authorize conferment of certain special powers upon members of the Armed Forces in disturbed areas. It is to be noted that the statute of 1958 has not been diluted or tinkered by any of the successive governments, whether of Congress or others. This is itself suggestive of its imperative need.

It is often commented that recourse to AFSPA should be left to the State administration rather than to the Central Government. It needs to be appreciated that it is a constitutional obligation of the Union of India to maintain unity and sovereignty of the nation[10]. In that view of the matter, deteriorating law and order situation may at some stage reach a state when the Governor or the Central

Government views the matter as disturbed or dangerous. In that contingency a notification by the Governor or the Central Government that the situation in that State or part thereof has worsened to an alarming level and turned disturbed or dangerous is required to be manifested in the form of a proclamation in the official gazette by way of a notification. This decision would then travel from Ministry of Human Affairs under whose domain is the responsibility of maintenance of law and order to the Ministry of Defence, empower to utilise Armed Forces who alone can actually make the forces available.

The provisions of AFSPA have been invoked for various durations in different North-Eastern states and in J&K. A challenge was made to this practice and to the legality of the above statutes in the case of Naga People's Movement of Human Rights V Union of India. [11] The petitioners assailed the legislation as a fraud on the Constitution and attacked it the grounds that the powers conferred on Armed Forces personnel under section 4 (a) of the Act were drastic, discriminatory and draconian.[12] It was further alleged that the Act was a colourable legislation and its enactment was a fraud perpetrated on the constitution. Seeking the assistance of the Armed Forces by the Union Government to control a disturbed situation was alleged to amount to handing over the power of maintenance of public order to the Armed Forces directly.

All these contentions were examined by the Supreme Court in its judgement which squarely upheld validity of the AFSPA. Yet in its judicial wisdom, the apex court introduced a few effective safeguards having due regard to the criticisms of the legislation. It was laid down that every notification invoking AFSPA would need to be reviewed before expiry of six months. By implication, such a relook could result in either the notification being retained for the complete area or being withdrawn with regard to the whole or a portion of the disturbed area. The Supreme Court pointed that it would be desirable for the Central Government to consult the State Government before issue of any notification. It was made clear that the Armed Forces were not to supplant or act as a substitute for the civil power because the State administration was to continue to function. Military was merely deployed to assist the State machinery to control the trouble some elements. Armed Forces personnel were directed to use minimum force while discharging their duties. It was made incumbent upon them to hand over arrested person within 24 hours to the nearest Police Station. Procedural safeguards incorporated under the Criminal Procedural Code[13] with regard to search and seizure were mandatory to be adhered. Supreme Court expected Armed Forces to co-opt women police while entering any household or other place having female inmates.

Lastly the Supreme Court directed that any order of the Central Government denying or permitting the prosecutions, suit or other legal proceeding against Armed Forces personnel would disclose reasons for the same. Thereby the order came to be liable to be examined and subjected to judicial scrutiny.

It would be significant to appreciate that while pronouncing of AFSPA, the Supreme Court proceeded to invest two additional powers on the Armed Forces personnel by necessary implications. The first was with regard to permission for interrogation of '*apprehendees*' by the military persons. The other allowed them to retain custody of the captured weapons. The latter was an operational necessity to prevent the arms being recycled for use by the militants.

A very significant part of the order related to introduction of notion of compensatory justice. Monetary compensation cannot undo the physical and mental trauma of violence causing bodily harm. Nevertheless, pecuniary amend may partially take the form of appearing as a solace and rehabilitation effort.

Notwithstanding the judicial position, as discussed above, AFSPA has continued to draw flaks from the Human Rights activists. Numerous instances are cited of atrocities on civilians at the hand of soldiers in Jammu & Kashmir and Manipur. It is often alleged that the provisions have been abused and misused by the military personnel. It is also stated that the civil population is harassed and made to suffer inconvenience at the hands of security personnel. Power given under section 4(a) to the Armed Forces personnel to use force to the extent of causing death has been particularly the target of vicious attack. Pointing out a few cases where military men were tried by courts martial for staging fake encounters to earn '*gallantary*' awards, it was alleged that in actual fact fake encounters did take place. Further there is considerable heart burn due to denial of sanction by the Central Governments in cases where the State administration had initiated proceedings for prosecution of military personnel for using excessive force. Prime Minister Dr Manmohan Singh has made an unambiguous announcement that the Act would be reviewed. This assurance has raised vast expectations that have remained unmet.

Any attempt to rephrase the clause pertaining to use of force to the extent of causing death has so far eluded any success. Should it be worded to say that force could be used but short of causing death? Or should the words 'causing of death' be totally deleted? Would it be operationally feasible to use force but altogether avoid any fatal casualty. Assuming such an attempt was to be made, what impact would it have on ongoing prosecutions against military personnel on charges of causing grievous injuries or otherwise excessive force while acting against anti national elements.

In this regard it may be pertinent to recall the words of the Supreme Court that "It must be remembered that merely because power may sometimes be abused, it is no ground for denying the existence of power. The wisdom of man has not yet been able to conceive of a government with power sufficient to answer all its legitimate needs and at the same time incapable of mischief."[14]

In conclusion, it would be prudent to attempt greater sensitisation of the Armed Forces Personnel to the Human Rights provisions. Such an effort could consist of improved training, dissemination, implementation and compliance. Better awareness can be brought about by introduction of specific courses for the rank and file at courses of instruction. Separate manuals can be provided for Human Rights and IHL provision to facilitate their proper dissemination to the defence forces. Actual adherence to Human Rights norms can be attained by designing imaginative war games, tactical exercises without troops (TWETs) and workshops. It may be fruitful to compile actual case studies to draw meaningful lessons. In the area of compliance, it is suggested that a probe must be obligatory in any incident involving death, grievous injury or which has given rise to an allegation of a sexual misconduct.

An investigation in any matter amounting to abuse of Human Rights must be investigated in a transparent manner by co-opting a civil official in the court of enquiry. Investigations must be completed in a time bound manner. Proceedings of such an investigation can be held at places easily accessible to civil witnesses. The probes in matters involving allegations of sexual misdemeanor must include a women officer as a member of the court of enquiry or in attendance. Military law provisions as contained in the Army Act can be amended to introduce an omnibus offence to include HR violations. Lastly, JAG Department Officers must be utilized in the process of recording of confessional statements, seizure memos and FIR etc.

End Notes

1. Articles 12 to 32

2. *Article 33. Power of Parliament to modify the rights conferred by this part in their application to Forces, etc. – Parliament may, by law, determine to what extent any* of the rights conferred by this part shall in their application to :-

   a) the members of the Armed Forces; or

   b) xxx

   c) xx

   d) xxx

be restricted or abrogated so as to ensure the proper discharge of their duties and the maintenance of discipline among them.

[3] Act 10 of 1994

[4] Section 14

[5] Sections 17 and 18

[6] Section 12

[7] Section 12 (c)

[8] Section 19

[9] Army Rule 177

[10] Ariticle 355. *Duty of the Union to protect States against external aggression and internal disturbance.* It shall be the duty of the Union to protect every State against external aggression and internal disturbance and to ensure that the Government of every State is carried on in accordance with the provisions of the Constitution.

[11] AIR 1998 SC 431

[12] Section 4. *Special Powers of the Armed Forces.* Any commissioned officer, warrant officer, non commissioned officer or any other person of equivalent rank in the Armed Forces may, in a disturbed area –

(a) if he is of opinion that it is necessary so to do for the maintenance of public order, after giving such due warning as he may consider necessary, fire upon or otherwise use force, even to the causing of death, against any person who acting in contravention of any law or order for the time being in force in the disturbed area prohibiting the assembly of five or more persons or the carrying of weapons or of things capable of being used as weapons or of fire arms, ammunition or explosive substances.

(b) xxx

(c) xxx

(d) xxx

[13] Act 5 of 1908

[14] State of Rajasthan V UOI; 1978(1) SCR 1

Session II : Second Paper

International Humanitarian Law – A Combat Leader's View

❑ Lieutenant General PC Katoch,PVSM,UYSM,AVSM,SC (Retd)

Upholding human rights and humanitarian laws are not new to India. Ancient Indian history describing the epic battles of Mahabharat era centuries ago make specific mention of humanitarian conduct during combat. In conflict situations including combating terrorism and insurgencies, the approach of the Indian Army has always been humane, people centric, upholding the law of the land, deep respect for human rights (HR) and minimum use of force avoiding collateral damage, for creating a secure environment. Upholding human dignity, personal values, fundamental rights, mitigation of public hardship are imbibed in all ranks through intensive training, motivation, stringent discipline and a layered command mechanism monitoring operations. The 'Ten Commandments' of the Chief of the Army Staff in this regard are carried in the pocket of every soldier. This is reinforced by essential values like secularism, discipline, integrity, loyalty, espirit-de-corps and an apolitical outlook. Ongoing operations in Afghanistan, parts of Pakistan and other conflict zones world over may be seen in sharp contrasts including consistent use of heavy weaponry disregarding collateral damage.

Our forces operate in an environment of extreme provocation, constant media glare and threat of human rights violations. In such an environment, even an inconsequential breach is rhetorically highlighted as human rights violation. Such allegations get further fuelled by large scale media coverage. Ironically, while actions of security forces are closely monitored by human rights watchdogs and NGOs, the same can hardly be said of the terrorists and militants whose blatant and heinous acts of violence and transgression are simply overlooked. Notwithstanding this, each allegation is transparently investigated jointly with police and representatives of the concerned civilian population and exemplary punishment awarded where culpability is established. As per our National Human Rights Commission (NHRC) figures only 4-5 per cent of allegations have proved true.

Much has been written on the relationship between International Humanitarian Law (IHL) and International Human Rights Law (IHRL). Both complement and strengthen each other. *IHL rules are intended to solve humanitarian problems directly arising from international or non-international armed conflicts; to protect persons and property that are, or may be, affected by an armed conflict and limits the rights of the parties to a conflict to use methods and means of warfare of their choice.* However, non-state actors and terrorist respect no laws and covenants and take recourse to overbearing brutality and ruthlessness in their actions while pursuing their nefarious goals. They have no compunctions in butchering or brutally maiming innocent civilians and security forces personnel.

Conflict situations in recent years have amply proved that asymmetric and irregular forces have greater strategic value over conventional and even nuclear forces. So, we are going to see more and more of this type of conflict. What is the applicability of IHL in such circumstances? Should the international community not address the issue?

In a situation of state sponsored terrorism, as India is contending with, shouldn't IHL apply and if so, how? When the LeT that is exclusively based in Pakistan besides being the covert arm of Pakistan Military-ISI combine, attacks India should this not be classified under the international conflict regime? Such issues need to be seriously addressed though viewing India as a convenient terror absorbing sponge by some does lead to intransigence.

Non-state actors do not figure in the prevalent humanitarian regimes simply under the argument that they are not 'organised entities' whose members can be held responsible for violations. This is absurd and an ostrich view. For example, surely the world does not want the Al Qaeda or the LeT to get 'more organised'. Why not take the bull by the horn or admit that the international community can do nothing about it. Judgements even in absentia are surely not a new concept.

Let me now come to some specific combat situations. Let us take the right to self defence. Does it include the right of 'pre-emptive self defence' and how does one define 'pre-emptive'? The LTTE was adept in using innocent civilians as 'human shields' especially when confronting security forces in open through built up areas; a trend which at times has surfaced in J&K. What do the security forces do? Take numerous casualties to own troops or fire in 'preventive self defence'? The militants / terrorists do this on purpose knowing casualties to civilians will be bonanza for a psychological media blitz. In this context, it is interesting to observe the following extracts of an address by Mr Amitabh Bachan to cadets of the National Defence Academy : *"The one that alarmed me most was the revelation, that, the army follows a given ethical code of warfare, even when they fight intruders. The insurgents do not wear uniform and therefore do not qualify as an army as such. But if they carry a weapon then the army has the right to attack them. However, the ethics in civilian war of this kind is that they are not to open fire until the enemy does so. So the forces wait in the most difficult terrain and circumstances till such act occurs. The other factor is that if the militant after opening fire were to drop his weapon, the army cannot attack him, for he, because of his disposition, then becomes a civilian and the civilian as per ethics of the armed forces cannot be attacked or fired upon. The ultimate results therefore are that the army become sitting ducks almost at the guile and mercy of the insurgent. The loss of personnel, officers and jawans of the forces then becomes an imminent factor for consideration. We lose our men in these grave circumstances, in excess of what they would, in fair and rightful warfare. What an unfair disadvantage !"*

Let us talk of conventional conflict. During the Kargil War. *Captain Saurabh Kalia and five other soldiers who were captured by Pakistani forces on 15 May 1999 were brutally tortured for 22 long days before they were shot, and their mutilated corpses delivered to India. "The postmortem revealed that the Pakistan Army had indulged in the most heinous acts; of burning their bodies with cigarettes, piercing ear-drums with hot rods, puncturing eyes before removing them, breaking most of the teeth and bones, chopping off various limbs and private organs of these soldiers besides inflicting all sorts of physical and mental tortures before shooting them dead, as evidenced by the bullet wound to the temple," says Wikipedia. In another case Squadron Leader Ajay Ahuja, whose MiG was shot down over Indian soil on 27 May 1999, was used for target practice by Pakistani soldiers after he bailed out and opened his parachute.* Though India lodged a strong protest with Pakistan, forget prosecution, not one Pakistani soldier responsible for these heinous acts was officially identified. Perhaps many of them were quietly given medals for these acts. To top it, not a whimper of protest by human rights groups and NGOs! Not even a small mention in the annual reports of the ACHR or any other HR organisation ! Incidentally, despite these barbaric acts of Pakistan, the Indian Army handed over the dead bodies of Pakistani soldiers in proper fashion. It is a different issue that the Pakistanis dumped the bodies unceremoniously in the dead of night at their next of kin's doorstep (as reported by Pakistan media) for fear of acknowledging these were soldiers from the Northern Light Infantry and not terrorists.

Stress on soldiers in combat situations of terrorism and insurgency requires little elaboration. How do you insulate him from unwarranted surmounting stress of false accusations of serious crimes like rape including ignominy during the attachments and long winded inquiries while media cries blue murder and tarnishes the image of individual (s) and the Army. Can you gauge the effect of undue additional stress levels caused by regular spate of false human rights abuse allegations (94-95 per cent as per NHCR) on soldiers in addition to combat stress? While I was posted at Srinagar as Colonel GS Operations during 1990-91, a village called Kushan Pushpora in Kupwara district was searched during winter on a night of continuous snow and rain, on receipt of information that one of the militants hiding there. More than one unit was involved. Three days 'after' the operation, DC Kupwara (under militant threat, militant sympathy or for money offered by militants) himself lodged an FIR that the Army had raped 100 women in that single night including a 60 year old woman. It created a national and international furore. What followed was a spate of commissions and inquiries, eventually all proving after a year plus that the allegations were totally baseless. Are human rights only linked to the 'physical' ?

Recently, in an equally sensational case related to the death of two women at Shopian in J&K, which kicked up great unrest, media frenzy and political skullduggery of the worst kind, charge of murder and rape was pinned on the security forces, later proved only as a case of drowning. The media too at times is under terrorist threat or is available on hire- which may be a global phenomenon. A former joint Director IB writes in his book 'Open Secrets', "*The susceptibility of the fourth estate to the intelligence community had tied our hands down. They are one of the too many holy Indian cows. Some of them, as described by a senior member of the fourth estate, 'taxi on hire'. Any paymaster can hire this particular brand.*" The essence of some of the rules of international humanitarian law and human rights law is similar. For example, both bodies of law aim to protect human life, prohibit torture or cruel treatment, prescribe basic rights for persons facing criminal proceedings and prohibit discrimination but what about mental torture? How do you protect soldiers from this? Should this not be addressed?

A Commanding Officer in J&K recently wrote to me, "*There was a recent incident which could have been blown up into human rights issue. An aged Kashmiri woman with her daughter walked into our soldiers sitting in ambush in a forest, while searching for 'gucchis' (type of mushroom). On spotting the soldiers she ran terrified for 100m, collapsed and died. Our medic tried to revive her but couldn't. Luckily the woman's daughter was witness. She appreciated our efforts and stood by us, preventing the militants to blow up the issue*". Another Commanding Officer writes, "*I feel that the Army is in a way protector of human rights in J&K rather than a violator. It is only after the normal law and order is restored and the civil administration functions under the popularly elected government, that basic human rights of the people can be ensured. In a larger perspective, these human rights issues are improved quality of life, opportunities of development, opportunities of education, health care and greater freedom in life*". Both IHL and IHRL require national implementation measures to make them reality but how do you implement it for non-state actors including state sponsored ones?

Due emphasis must given to human rights of soldiers especially when in combating-insurgency and terrorism (including state sponsored) they are doing extremely difficult tasks on behalf of the state. If they fail, the state would wither away. Can you let that happen? Having said this much, I would like to pose a question to you: Are Soldiers Human? Apparently there is a doubt since this is the very title of a workshop being organised by the University of Manchester on 24 September 2010. *One of the issues to be discussed is "How are soldiers treated as human 'material', and what constraints are posed by their humanity? Do soldiers become human only after death, in their memorialisation"?* The fact is that the inability of the IHL, IHRL, human rights organisations and connected NGOs to address non-state actors (including state sponsored ones) puts undue stress on soldiers fighting a 'dirty war'. It would not be wrong to say that this amounts to inadvertent catalyst for terrorists and militants to violate human rights with impunity. The global community also needs to seriously consider expanding the scope of the IHL and IHRL in providing protection to every global citizen for growing up 'humans' which should be his / her basic human right. An opinion in the Daily Times of Pakistan dated 11 May 2009 read, *"There are thousands of madrassas spread all over Pakistan's urban centres that are producing millions of neo-drones ... Take a little boy and incarcerate him in a remote madrassa. Indoctrinate him with a distorted version of a religion and tell him that he does not belong to this world. Teach him about the fanciful world that awaits him in the heaven and that in order to attain that he has to destroy everything that stands in his way, including his own body...... At full steam ahead in Pakistan, this is a monstrous experiment in brainwashing and it is on a par with, if not worse than, Nazi Germany's eugenics. They did it in the name of science; here, it is being done in the name of God and religion. On a very large scale, this is a hugely successful experiment in which nurture triumphs and nature takes a beating".*

If due cognisance of above violation of what should be the basic right of every individual is taken by the international community and due measures instituted, we may then prevent proliferation of neo drones and engage the scourge of terrorism on better footing. Otherwise aliens from outer space may well descend to destroy the human race before we destroy this planet. It may also put a curb on blasphemic statements of national leaders like former Pakistani dictator and President, General

Pervez Musharraf declaring to global international audiences through electronic media that there is not a single terrorist on Pakistani soil.

I have not touched on issues like practical problems of implementation of IHL in a theatre of operation where international obligations of States participating in the same international military operation (like Afghanistan) differ in interpretation of IHL. I have restricted myself to what concerns the soldier in combat. I admit that some may find these views perhaps blunt and not strictly within the purview of the ICRC. However, should this set the tone for some to don their thinking caps, I will consider myself lucky.

Session II - Discussion (Q & A)

Issues Raised

How can the Armed Forces (Special Powers) Act (AFSPA) be modified for making it '*people friendly*'; without "*lowering the morale of our troops*" or without reducing the legal cover it provides to 'enable' them to function decisively and expeditiously against anti-national elements, who neither have any ethics nor constraints on them ?

Responses

(a) Firstly, the Indian army should be complimented for the role they have played in upholding of human rights in J&K.

(b) Strangely, nobody has done enough to publicise that AFSPA gives no more power to the Armed Forces than what is available to the Police under the IPC 1860 and the CrPC, 1973. It has also not been highlighted that the Army follows the guidelines of the Honourable Supreme Court and obeys the 'Do's' and 'Don'ts' laid down by the Chief of Army Staff. There is a general misapprehension that this Act provides some kind of extraordinary powers to the Indian Armed Forces – this misunderstanding of the AFSPA must be removed.

(c) The Indian Army has taken disciplinary action against many defaulters under the stringent provisions of the Indian Army Act to deal with heinous crimes involving human right violations during CI operations in disturbed areas, covered by the AFSPA. These actions should have been publicised and kept on the website to inform people that serious violations of human rights by Army personnel are dealt with swiftly and decisively. Nobody condones such crimes or wilful disobedience of orders in the Army. The provisions of the Army Act 1950 ensure that the Army personnel do not violate the fundamental or human rights of any citizen guaranteed by the Constitution of India.

(d) All the criticism against the Armed Forces is being voiced because people generally do not know that such a system exists and works with notable efficiency under the watchful eyes of the Judge Advocate General Department and the Adjutant General of the Army.

(e) The time-tested system of the Armed Forces to deal with delinquent acts of indiscipline works with utmost urgency and best intent. Violations of good order and military discipline under the provisions of Section 63 of the Indian Army Act 1950, is the most frequently invoked Section of the Army Act. In fact, that is what helps the Army to maintain its high standards of discipline, both, during 'peace' and 'active' operations.

(f) Aberrant behaviour on the part of a few individuals, which tarnish the image of the Army as a whole, and undermine the good work done by almost everyone else, is effectively dealt with by the Army's in-house mechanism. It is sad that the people are not aware of the trials carried out through Army Summary and General Court Martials to deal with all acts of omission and commission, which have surfaced periodically.

(g) The mischievous propaganda by anti-national elements and sometimes even by well meaning people, that Armed Forces personnel are not 'people friendly', strengthens and emboldens the insurgents to take advantage of it. It has to be noted that the Army has a different way of doing things, which leaves little room for mistakes. People are unaware of this aspect also. The Army's zeal for efficiency and despatch is sometimes misconstrued as ruthlessness. Their normal conduct and actions are not governed by the AFSPA. This aspect needs understanding and propagation all around. There is no good reason for the Army to conceal either the crimes or the follow up disciplinary actions against such individuals.

(h) Whatever mechanisms the Armed Forces are applying to deal with *'violation of human rights',* cases should be brought into the public domain, to make them transparent. The media should be taken into confidence to prevent misinterpretation of incidents. This step would check exaggerated and mischievous reporting by interested parties.

(j) An objective study of the Armed Forces role in CI operations requires legal comprehension of the relevant articles and provisions of the Constitution of India, the Armed Forces (Special Powers) Act, 1958; Protection of Human Rights Act, 1993 and the provisions of the Army Act, 1950.

(k) The AFSPA is a legal empowerment of the Army to enable it to carry out its duties efficiently, and to provide legal cover to its personnel against malafide, motivated and unsubstantiated allegations. It is applicable only in the insurgency affected areas, where the State government and the Police are unable to control the *'law and order'* situation, compelling it to declare the area as 'disturbed' – which clears the way for the induction of the Army by the Central Government, for the restoration of law and order in the specified area. The provisions of AFSPA become applicable only when the Army is deployed in such 'Disturbed Areas' to do a 'police' job, to help the law abiding citizens to lead a normal life. During this secondary role, they are simply given a legal cover through the AFSPA provision, to enable them to carry out their duties in a domain that is different from their primary role.

(l) The AFSPA statutes have also been examined by the Supreme Court, in response to a petition challenging their legality; specially the provisions under Section 4 (a). The Supreme Court upheld its validity after careful legal scrutiny of the whole Act.

Issue Raised

Since early 1990s, media reports all over the country have implied that the Indian Army carries out all the security related operations in disturbed areas. This is a wrong perception. Such mis-reporting tarnishes the image of the Armed Forces, who are mostly engaged in military operations to guard the international borders. *What can be done to reassure the Armed Forces that services being rendered by them during CI operations under statutory provisions of the Indian legal system are seen and reported in the right perspective?*

Response

(a) Firstly, the media should not mix up the actions carried out for the maintenance of 'law and order' in a disturbed area, with CI operations conducted by the Army. Secondly, maintenance of 'Law and Order' is a State subject and responsibility, which it is required to discharge with its own Police forces. It is first augmented on request with Central Police Forces (CPOs), like the CRPF, BSF, ITBP,and RAF etc, by the Central Government. The Armed Forces are brought in as an *'Aid to Civil Power,'* only when the State administration and the CPOs have failed and are unable to handle the worsening law and order situation effectively. The media should project this distinction clearly while reporting such incidents.

(b) The use of distinctive uniforms – by the State Police, Central Police Forces and the Military should be strictly enforced. For example, the *'combat dress'* should be worn only by the Army personnel. It would then have a salutary effect on the civil population to warn them, that hereafter, the Army will not allow them to continue with their unlawful activities.

(c) It is important that the '*ethos*' of the Armed Forces, of their being the 'Nation's *pride*' is maintained because they are the '*instrument of last resort*'. Nothing should be done to dilute their efficiency or their resolve to succeed under all circumstances. That is the spirit, which motivates them to sacrifice their lives while performing their duty.

Issue Raised

In all their fundamental rules and the covenants, IHL and the Geneva Conventions use the word '*armed forces*' generically or effectively. In this way the '*Police and the CPOs*' are also a party to the resolution of a conflict. In the same context, *what position do the private security organisations like Blackwater in Iraq enjoy during armed conflicts?*

Response

(a) IHL was designed in the aftermath of World War II. At that time, there were no PMFs or CPOs to undertake these sorts of roles. The term '*armed forces*' is therefore, used generically. However, some other words, for example '*unlawful*' combatants or militia, do find a mention in that context.

(b) Presently, another thing, which is receiving the attention of IHL, is the '*role and status of civilians*' in the conflict zone. After the Iraq and Afghanistan Wars, the ICRC has set up an expert group to determine whether the large number of '*civilians who are not in uniform and are yet drawn in the conflict zone*' are entitled to protection under the IHL.

(c) Presently, the status of organisations like Blackwater is not clear. However, the issue is under consideration and some policy directions may evolve in the future.

Issue Raised

There is an indication and feeling that the terrorists should not have human rights. What is the legal position in this regard?

Response

The legal position on this aspect is very clear. For example, every Indian has seen 'Kasab do what he did in Mumbai' but it does not mean that he does not deserve a fair trial. One of the basic notions of a criminal trial is that an accused is presumed to be innocent till proved otherwise. The onus of doing so rests on the prosecution. The ingredients of the charges framed against him have to be proved beyond all reasonable doubt. This is the reason why even Kasab's trial has taken months. There is no doubt that all legal rights, in our context *'Fundamental Rights',* are available even to a convict, unless 'a right' is specifically denied to him. For example, the inmates in a jail do not have the right to travel freely.

Session III

International Humanitarian Law as Applicable in the 21st Century

Chairman	-	Mr François Stamm, HoRD of the ICRC in Delhi
Speakers	-	Mr Chris Harland, ICRC Legal Adviser in the New Delhi Delegation of the ICRC
	-	Maj Gen AJS Sandhu, VSM (Retd)

Chairman's Opening Remarks

❑ Mr Francois Stamm, HoRD of the ICRC in India

I have hinted in my introductory remarks that the ICRC firmly believes that IHL is relevant and remains applicable in the 21st Century. I also said that we welcome different views and we invite, more importantly, a debate around this notion. I think it is important that IHL is not seen as a static body of law. It is evolving, of course; IHL must also evolve. The ICRC wants to be part of this debate and again we thank the USI and all the participants for coming today to participate in this debate. Our first speaker is Chris Harland. You know him very well, he has been working here at the ICRC Regional Delegation in New Delhi for nearly three years now. He is our regional legal adviser for South Asia, based in New Delhi. His responsibilities include working with governments in the region i.e. the SAARC countries to ensure that their international obligations under IHL are reflected in their domestic legal order. He was, before coming to Delhi, with the Legal Division at our Geneva Headquarters. As a Canadian Lawyer, he has over 12 years of experience in conflict and post-conflict environment in Africa, Europe and Asia. He has worked not only with the ICRC for a long time but also for the United Nations.

Session III – First Paper

❑ Mr Christopher Harland, ICRC Regional Legal Adviser for South Asia

In this presentation, I hope to briefly cover some new challenges and developments in International Humanitarian Law, or IHL. Following a bit of background, I will highlight where the ICRC feels today's IHL can and should develop.

But before I do that I think it is important to mention that many of the traditions that inspired today's IHL actually come from this part of the world, and from Asia more generally. For example, the first commonly noted written expression of IHL comes from Jiang Taigong's Six Secret Teachings in China, which is over 3000 years old. This includes expressions that find reflection in today's IHL, for example, military orders respecting gravesites and altars and persons not directly participating in hostilities. Today's rules may be slightly different, but they find inspiration in the same places. Although we date modern IHL from the battle of Solferino in 1859, and from the First Geneva Convention in 1864, the ideas, the inspirations behind these provisions find expression in many ancient cultures and traditions including those of the sub-continent such as the Mahahbharata, and the Code of Manu.

Before discussing current challenges, I propose to offer some of the most important elements of IHL. Then, I plan to offer a few ideas concerning current challenges faced in IHL and mention a couple of recent developments on the weapons front which may be of interest to this audience. I will then touch briefly, assuming we have time, on national implementation and where India stands, and where there might be some future work that might be considered.

I therefore begin with what is IHL, or the law of armed conflict. When we at ICRC speak of IHL, we essentially mean the rules found in 100 treaties and related documents, but we concentrate on 28 main treaties as well as customary international law. The 28 main treaties can be grouped into a number of categories, as follows.

The first is "protection". Protection refers to the protection of those not taking part in hostilities or who are no longer taking part in hostilities. This includes, for example, rules in the 1949 Geneva Conventions and the 1977 Additional Protocols, as well as the 1954 Cultural Property Convention. The second is weapons, and includes, for example, the Chemical Weapons Convention, the 1980 Convention on Certain Conventional Weapons and its five protocols, and the recent Convention on Cluster Munitions. A third category is enforcement, including the prohibitions in the International Criminal Court, which has war crimes provisions in it. Similarly, the "grave breaches" provisions of the Four Geneva Conventions of 1949 and the first Additional Protocol of 1977 include prohibitions which each State party should criminalise. A fourth category includes customary international humanitarian law, which binds states even if it has not necessarily been codified. Efforts to do so culminated in the 2005 publication of the ICRC Study on Customary International Humanitarian Law. There are also other treaties which are not "pure" IHL treaties but have some links to IHL. For example, this includes the Genocide Convention, the Convention Against Torture and the International Covenant on Civil and Political Rights, violations of which, if conducted in war time, may also amount to war crimes. The same is true for the recent Enforced Disappearances Conventions, with a link between that treaty and the provisions on missing persons that you would find for example in the Additional Protocols of 1977 and in customary IHL rules.

IHL applies in times of armed conflict, whereas human rights apply in both peace and armed conflict. However, many human rights may be derogated from in times of emergency. In addition, the International Court of Justice (among others) has indicated that in times of armed conflict, IHL is "lex specialis" or specialised law, which takes some measure of precedence over human rights law. While IHL applies only in times of armed conflict, it must be prepared for in times of peace. This includes, for example, adopting appropriate implementing legislation, ensuring that military manuals comply with IHL, and in translating international conventions into official languages.

There are two main types of armed conflict – international and non-international. International armed conflict applies between two or more States parties to the Geneva Conventions, occurring on the territory of a State Party. The Four Geneva Conventions of 1949 then apply, as does the 1977 First Additional Protocol. Occupation law is a subset of international armed conflict, and it applies "to all cases of partial or total occupation of the territory of a High Contracting Party, even if the said occupation meets with no armed resistance." (GC IV, art. 2).

Non-international armed conflict, the second type of armed conflict, is "protracted armed violence" that occurs on the territory of a State Party, and requires both a high level of intensity of the violence, and sufficient command and organisation of the armed groups party to the conflict. When this is reached, both common Article 3 to the 1949 Geneva Conventions, as well as the 147 rules of the customary law study which are applicable in non-international armed conflict, will apply. Further rules in Additional Protocol II require that the armed groups hold territory and that the conflict include government forces.

At the end of hostilities, there may still exist obligations which relate to the conflict, for example, the obligation to return prisoners of war, or to ensure that those tried for war crimes are given judicial guarantees provided for under IHL.

Under current challenges of IHL, I want to speak briefly about a project that the ICRC started about a year ago, announced at the 60th anniversary of the 1949 Geneva Conventions. For information, the 61st anniversary is tomorrow, the 12th of August. Last August, the ICRC President announced that the ICRC was starting a project that in French goes by the name CANI+, in English it might be NIAC or Non-International Armed Conflict Plus. As mentioned earlier, many of the customary law rules, which bind states, are not currently reflected in treaty law, at least as far as non-international armed conflict is concerned. The ICRC is therefore looking to see whether there is support for the adoption of new treaty-based rules which might apply in NIAC. The customary law study mentioned earlier, has just been made public on our website, all 5000 pages of it, and in a well-organised form, so I would recommend anyone interested in further study consult it. The CANI+ project intends to turn some of the NIAC rules into treaty form.

For the ICRC, therefore, one current challenge to IHL is the non-existence in treaty form of important rules in non-international armed conflict, which we hope to work on in the coming years.

A further development is the publication of the ICRC's Interpretive Guidance on the Notion of Direct Participation in Hostilities, including 10 recommendations and 90 pages of commentary. This sets out for the ICRC the conditions under which a civilian, who is normally legally protected from direct attack, may lose this protection, as a result of his or her direct participation in hostilities. Such civilians still benefit from the general rules of IHL such as precautions in attack, proportionality etc, military necessity. Again, this information is available on our website.

Another future area of study for the ICRC is the legal test of proportionality. This is important because arms bearers need to be able to be clearer when they may attack a military target and when they may not. Proportionality is a balancing test between the expected concrete and direct military advantage to be gained by an attack and, on the other hand, the expected loss to civilian life and property when combined. If the balance favours the latter, the attack must not be undertaken. We hope that we will be able to provide further elements of the test following further internal study.

We are also looking the elements of the definition of armed conflict, non-international in particular, which will help States in determining when an armed conflict exists, beyond the information contained in the ICRC's March 2008 Opinion Paper on the subject.

Further, we are updating the ICRC commentary to the Four Geneva Conventions and the Three Protocols over the next few years.

On weapons, I would mention three developments. The first is the recent entry into force of the Convention on Cluster Munitions. Cluster munitions now kill or injure more people than anti-personnel landmines do worldwide. We encourage States to consider becoming a party to this Convention, which has now reached the number of ratifications necessary for entry into force.

The second is the ICRC's April 2010 public statement relating to nuclear weapons. This follows on from UN Security Council Resolution 1887 of September last year in which States noted the need to try to work towards a world without nuclear weapons. The ICRC's position is to support negotiations in the drafting of a legally binding instrument to eliminate nuclear weapons. We know that this is not going to happen overnight.

I would also mention that there is work in the United Nations on the Arms Trade Treaty (ATT). The ICRC's position on the ATT which is now being negotiated, is that it should be a comprehensive global treaty that defines binding standards for transfers of small arms and light weapons. This builds on States' responsibilities, including those under IHL. In essence, this boils down to not selling small arms and light weapons to a group or state which would likely violate IHL with those weapons. The ICRC also argues that ammunition should be included in such a treaty, as well as issues related to brokering and transfers through third parties.

As compared with other countries in South Asia, India has made good efforts in legislating obligations flowing from international agreements, through legislation including the 1960 Geneva Conventions Act, the 2000 Chemical Weapons Act and the 2005 Weapons of Mass Destructions Act which also prohibits biological weapons. However, compared to other countries in the region, there are a number of international instruments which India could consider acceding to.

There may also be further consideration of legislative provisions relating to the Child Soldiers Protocol to the Convention on the Rights of the Child, as there is a requirement make a criminal offence of rebel groups recruiting child soldiers, as well as provisions relating to both cultural property and the Convention on Certain Conventional Weapons, specifically its amended Protocol II.

For further information on all of these issues, I would recommend visiting our website, www.icrc.org, as well as our library at Regional Delegation in Sunder Nagar, Delhi. Once again, many thanks to the United Services Institution for collaboration on this useful seminar.

Session III : Second Paper

❑ **Major General AJS Sandhu, VSM (Retd)**

Introduction

Definition. I shall commence my talk by re-calling the definition of International Humanitarian Law (IHL). "IHL is a body of rules, established by treaty or custom, which for humanitarian reasons, *limits the right of parties* to a conflict *to use methods and means of warfare* of their choice; and *protects persons and property* that are, or may be affected by the conflict." IHL, also called the *Law of Armed Conflict* or the *Law of War*, neither bans war nor does it in any way affect the legal status of the parties to the conflict – it only concerns itself with the protection of the people affected by the war. Thus it becomes applicable when conflict begins, and ceases when conflict ends.

However, today one is faced with new forms of waging war, wherein the boundaries of IHL are being tested to the extreme. For example : How does one exactly define Non-International Armed Conflict or how does one decide that a 'conflict has begun' or that 'it has ended' ? How do you define the present situation existing in Iraq ? Thus, it becomes difficult to apply IHL, and the parties concerned tend to take advantage by selective interpretation of rules.

Development of IHL

It is necessary to briefly recapitulate the origins and further development of IHL till the 20th Century, as it has a bearing on the 21st Century context.

Although the principles of IHL existed even in ancient times, its formal codification started only after the founding of ICRC in 1863, which resulted in the *'First Geneva Convention of 1864'* dealing with the protection of sick / wounded soldiers. Thereafter, through the second half of the 19th Century and the period up to the Second World War, at a series of Conferences held at Geneva & Hague, additional treaties and conventions were formulated - based on the experiences gained in the wars fought during that period. It needs to be noted that all conflicts were 'international' in nature i.e. fought between individual Sovereign States or Coalition of States. The first half of the 20th Century saw the waging of two World Wars, with the attendant sufferings of prisoners, civilians as well as property. The experiences of the Second World War led to the convening of a diplomatic Conference which came up with an updated version of the Four Geneva Conventions of 1949, which till today form the foundation of IHL.

The post World War II period saw a surge of 'armed independence' struggles in Africa, Asia, South America & so on. Furthermore, advent of new technology resulted in the invention of even more lethal weapons. Thus a need was felt to re-affirm and further develop to keep pace with the changed environment. This resulted in the two Additional Protocols of 1977. In the 19th & 20th Centuries Sovereign States were either involved fighting one another (i.e. international armed conflicts) or the armies of Sovereign States fought against cohesive, well organised & armed guerilla armies of 'freedom fighters'. In the 21st Century – we are faced with other forms of 'enemies' such as Non-State Armed Groups, and hence the current debate i.e. "Can IHL be applied in these conflicts in its present form and content ?"

Reasons for the Ongoing Debate on Applicability of IHL in the 21st Century

The basic reasons for the present debate are as follows:-

(a) The 21st Century has seen a paradigm shift in the nature of conflict.

(b) Emergence of Non-State Armed Groups (as parties to conflict)

(c) Perceived inadequacy of IHL.

I shall now examine the applicability of IHL in the contemporary context by taking the example of some recent conflicts:-

(a) Afghanistan / Iraq

(b) Israel – Lebanon Conflict (2006)

(c) Sri Lanka – LTTE Conflict

This is best achieved by analysing whether the five Basic Principles of IHL (which are indeed the essence of IHL) were adhered to by the parties involved in above – mentioned conflicts.

Principles of IHL

The Basic Principles of IHL are:-

(a) Limitation

(b) Distinction

(c) Military necessity

(d) Proportionality

(e) Humanity

War In Iraq / Afghanistan. Let us first take a look at the recent wars fought against Iraq & Afghanistan, which have been grouped together. There are numerous examples of violations of IHL, but I have picked only a few:-

(a) Civilian targets.

(b) Maltreatment of prisoners.

(c) Use of harsh interrogation techniques.

Israeli – Lebanon Conflict (2006):-

(a) Attacks on civilians

(b) Indiscriminate use of cluster munitions

(c) Misuse of civilian facilities

Sri Lanka – LTTE Conflict:-

(a) Civilian targets

(b) Use of disproportionate force

(c) Holding of hostages

India and Human Rights / Humanitarian Laws

The 'spirit of humanity' in times of war, has been a part of the Indian ethos, culture & tradition since ancient times. But in the current context, India's commitment to IHL / Human Rights can be gauged from the following :-

(a) Is a founder member of the United Nations Organisation (UNO)

(b) Original signatory of the UNDHR (1948).

(c) Original signatory of the 1949 Geneva Conventions (One of the earliest ratifiers).

(d) Gave legal sanction by enacting 'Geneva Conventions Act 1960.

(e) Has strictly adhered to Geneva Conventions in all conflicts

(f) Is a signatory to important international treaties / conventions

(g) India has a very strong Constitution.

1971 Indo – Pak War. Although, India has always abided by the Principles of IHL in all its post-Independence conflicts, it is the 1971 Indo – Pak war which best exemplifies India's adherence to IHL. This was a large scale, two front war at the end of which 92,000 Pakistani POWs were held in captivity for a long period. They were treated well, by the book both during and after the conflict in POW Camps in India.

Challenges

It is evident from the above examples that IHL has been characterised more by breach than compliance in the recent conflicts. Although, it continues to be relevant, it faces the following challenges :-

(a) Selective interpretation of rules by the parties engaged in a conflict.

(b) Increased use of private security contractors

(c) Problems in implementation / enforcement

(d) Inadequate dissemination & training

Conclusion

It is quite obvious that the IHL continues to be as relevant in the 21st Century as it has been in the past 150 years. However, in the context of present day conflict situations, some grey areas remain, which give ample room for 'selective interpretation'. The ICRC is seized with this matter, and some draft papers are under formulation to further reinforce and clarify various articles.

Chairman's Closing Remarks

I am grateful to both speakers, who gave very interesting and complementary presentations. I fully agree with your judgement, regarding appropriate judicial guarantees for the 'detainees', especially in the early days of their captivity. I would also clarify the point about the Guantanamo detainees, the ICRC did have access to these persons as soon as they were transferred to Cuba.

We have a little time to take a few questions.

Session III - Discussion (Q & A)

Issues Raised

Nowadays, we have this Universal Periodic Review (UPR) of the Human Rights Council every three months, which monitors observance of IHL and Human Rights Law. That is well settled. However, the real challenge lies in making these non-state actors, which form part of criminal and terrorists groups, adhere to the IHL. It is also a fact that they do appear in organised form and change their names when they are designated as terrorist groups. Since, they do have a command and control system: *How can we make them conscious of observing IHL, because they indulge in hostage taking and subject innocent people to extreme forms of torture ? In this context, what is the proposed methodology to deal with organisations like the erstwhile LTTE, Hezbollah, LeT etc in the 21st Century; and also with groups like Blackwater which are operating on behalf of the USA?*

Responses

(a) The Universal Periodic Review (UPR) covers Human Rights Law and not IHL. In 1985, there was a proposal to set up a UPR system under IHL but this was rejected by the USA. They suggested that such a thing could form a part of the ICRC's work. In that sense, the ICRC is able to have discussions with some groups, but finds it difficult to make contact with others. We succeeded in establishing appropriate contacts with some of them by meeting them in captivity i.e. we meet them in prisons, whenever we can. For example, in India we can have discussion with the detainees.

(b) There is a difference with respect to the status of contractors and civilians who follow along in international armed conflicts and non-international armed conflicts. Under *international armed conflicts*, the Geneva Conventions, Rule No 4 sets out who is a prisoner of war (POW); *not only the combatants but the civilians who follow along with the Army are also POWs.* So when they are captured they get the status of a POW but they cannot be targeted the way combatants are. Therefore, there are limits to the concessions that they can get but they are treated as POW.

Issue Raised

Some non-state actors undergo punishments and are legally entitled to fight against their convictions. It is not clear whether the ICRC interacts with such loose characters to document their views. A documented proof of their views could help in deciding whether such non-state actors should be entitled to enjoy protection under IHL and HR laws, always. *Is the ICRC engaged in evolving some strategy and policy for the future?*

Response

(a) There is a document which sets out the '*way*' for the ICRC, along with a number of states, to identify best practices which could help to impose some measure of control on the non-state actors.

(b) Practically, there is nothing on this subject, which could help the ICRC to make a distinction between the categories of non-state actors and to identify who amongst them would either be entitled to or not entitled to protection under IHL and HR laws.

(c) This is an interesting proposition, which with a little more experience, might receive the attention of the ICRC to evolve some measures in this regard.

Session IV

21st Century IHL Integration into the Armed Forces: The P5 Countries Experience– (Focusing on the USA and the Russian Federation)

Chairman	-	Lt Gen Randhir K Mehta, PVSM,AVSM,YSM,VSM (Retd)
Speakers	-	Mr Aleardo Ferretti, Coordinator for ICRC Relations with the US Armed Forces
	-	Brig Gen (Retd) William Bowie, Regional Delegate to the Armed and Security Forces of India

Chairman's Opening Remarks

❑ Lieutenant General RK Mehta, PVSM,AVSM,YSM,VSM (Retd)

In the Indian Army, we get exposed to IHL at the Cadet stage in the military academies. The treatment of 93,000 Pakistan POW's in 1971-72 is an example of good application of IHL by the Indian Armed Forces.

Aim of Military Programmes. The training programmes ensure that IHL is integrated into the armies and security forces (SF), both in theory and practice. Ideally, every soldier should know his responsibilities in the event of a conflict situation. He should also be protected by observance of the basic rules of IHL. Basically, implementation of IHL within Armed Forces is the responsibility of the country concerned.

IHL also has ongoing prevention programmes, with cooperation between armies and security forces throughout the world. It has two components – military and political.

When the UN came into being in 1945, there was only one nuclear power (the USA) - out of the five permanent members of the Security Council. Today, all five permanent members are nuclear powers. The Peoples Liberation Army (PLA) has undergone rapid modernisation in the past decade. The USA, UK and France are allied in different ways through NATO/EU. The USA and the UK Armed Forces have an expeditionary role.

A few thoughts on the P5 countries:-

(a) **Russia.** I expect Brigadier General Bowie to touch upon their flagship activities, the Russian-Chechen conflict of 1994-96 and in 1999, as also the Russia-Georgia-South Ossetia conflict with focus on genocide, crimes against humanity and war crimes in non-international and international armed conflicts. Rape as a weapon of war cannot be ignored. Since Brigadier General Bowie has been actively involved on behalf of the ICRC, I shall not highlight any other issues at this stage.

(b) **USA.** The USA has asserted that 'War on Terror' is an International armed conflict, even when it is not a conflict between states, where the territorial boundaries of the conflict are undefined, where the beginnings are amorphous and the end indefinable, especially when non-state parties are unspecified and indefinable entities that are not entitled to belligerent status. In the US view, there are no POWs in the Global War on Terror. No detainee is entitled to POW status. General Petreaeus, the new Commander of the US Forces in Afghanistan, has stated, "We must continue our emphasis on reducing the loss of innocent civilian lives to an absolute minimum. We must never forget the divisive terrain *in Afghanistan is* the human terrain". The USA , Russia and China are not signatories to the Cluster Bomb Ban – 01 Aug 2010.

I shall leave the details to Mr A Ferrati.

(c) **The UK**. The UK is a member of NATO and the EU. They have a love-hate relationship with the ICRC and consider it 'meddlesome' – as viewed by military men. They are unsure and uncertain in relation to the War on Terror and the challenges posed for the UK's foreign policy in terms of its obligations under IHL. The UK aims to coordinate its defence policies with allies and how to balance IHL considerations with its present security concerns. The impact of domestic laws and the policy on military operations poses a significant challenge as the UK's global role remains.

(d) **France.** France is presently engaged as part of EU operations in CHAD and the Central African Republic on behalf of the UN. It stresses that it is there to provide protection to innocent civilians. Such protection must involve primarily a guarantee of adherence to the principles of IHL in Armed Conflict and the inclusion of Protection of Civilians (PoC) in Peacekeeping Mandates. Its stand is amplified by the following:-

(i) On 29 Jan 2009 Mr Bernard Kouchner, Minister of Foreign and European Affairs stated, "Compliance with IHL must be made the subject of depoliticised discussions at the UN, since such compliance is the duty of all, irrespective of the legitimacy of the military action undertaken by a specific state or armed groups."

(ii) Referring to the Gaza conflict, he stated, this is not a humanitarian imperative; violations of the law significantly exacerbates situations in armed conflicts by making reconciliation more difficult and generating long term traumas in society.

(e) **China.** They have initiated major steps since 2005. In the spirit of the UN General Assembly Resolution 61/30, China is focusing on international cooperation and domestic institution building. China set up an ICRC office in Beijing in 2005. In Nov 2007, they established the National Committee of IHL. In April 2009, they established the PLA Liaison Institute of Legal Affairs.

Conclusions

(a) Ideas and debates on IHL and HR should include the Armed Forces Leadership; if not, the debate can become 'uninformed'.

(b) IHL has been criticised for not anticipating armed conflicts in the context of modern terrorism (this is between a state and one or more trans-national armed groups).

(c) Existing laws are considered a hindrance by many nations. It is proposed that when law and ground reality clash, it is the law that must give way.

(d) IHL should also adopt provisions to cover the so-called 'new forms of conflict'. This perhaps calls for the expansion of the concept of Armed Conflict or expansion of the scope of application of IHL beyond armed conflict. Use of drones, cyber warfare and its impact on the conduct of armed conflicts and the use of directed energy weapons are areas needing greater attention by the ICRC.

(e) IHL has continued relevance along with human rights law, despite it being considered meddlesome and being viewed with cynicism and scepticism by many nations. The ICRC has to rise to the new challenges arrising out of new wars / threats.

(f) IHL is basically fine; its boundaries are properly drawn in a respectful balance with the over-arching interests of state security, individual security and civil liberties. IHL is effective when properly implemented.

Session IV : First Paper

The ICRC and Relations with the US Armed Forces : An Overview of the Past Five Years of Interaction

❑ **Mr Aleardo Ferretti, ICRC Senior Delegate to the Armed Forces, Washington DC, USA**

Background and Evolution

The International Committee of the Red Cross (ICRC) interacts with the armed forces of over 100 countries on a regular basis as part of its mandate through the universally ratified four Geneva Conventions of 1949 on the implementation of international humanitarian law (IHL). Dialogue with armed forces is a natural and vitally important part of ICRC operating procedures, with a view to gaining the required levels of acceptance for its activities in favour of victims during a situation of armed conflict. The relationship between the ICRC and the US military falls within this framework and has been characterised over the years by varied levels of engagement, frequency and interaction. From occasional contacts, to more regular and systematic interaction, there currently exists significant institutionalised relations, touching different aspects of military policy and the operational planning and executive level.

The ICRC has long recognised the global reach of the US Armed Forces, and their participation or interest in conflicts where ICRC will also be present. Following the important and constructive interface between the ICRC and the US forces during the first Gulf War in 1991, with its conventional warfare characteristics and speedy resolution of the conflict, the interaction in the past eight years has been re-defined by the events of 9/11 and its consequences. The US military engagement in Afghanistan in 2001 and Iraq in 2003, with their respective aftermaths and humanitarian challenges, have led to a robust interaction with the ICRC. The Department of Defense (DoD) is an extremely important reference point for the

ICRC in the Administration.

Humanitarian issues related to the fight against terrorism and Guantanamo were at the heart of the post 9/11 discussions. This created a momentum, starting in 2003/2004, for the ICRC to engage deeper with the US Armed Forces active in theater, as well as the ones in the continental USA. Since 2004, an ICRC delegate has been dedicated to relations with the US Armed Forces, based in Washington DC. Since 2007, this has been increased to two delegates. This has created dedicated outreach to the US Armed Forces institutions for doctrine, training and education, as well as the combat training Centres. The approach has helped bolster recognition and augment knowledge of each others activities in a conflict situation, and further enhance the practical interaction at field level.

The ICRC and US Military Relationship

The United States Armed Forces remain actively engaged in different parts of the world. Inevitably, the US Armed Forces and the International Committee of the Red Cross (ICRC) have come to share theatres of operations, although the extent of the ICRC presence in each varies from some of its largest field operations in Afghanistan and Iraq to a more limited presence in other parts of the world. However, what is common in all of these contexts is the fact that the ICRC is involved in a regular and multi-faceted dialogue with the US personnel at various levels of command. This dialogue may simply include information and analysis sharing, such as on humanitarian concerns or needs, as well as on security issues. However, it may also be more specific and dynamic, extending to such issues as visits to detainees, the protection of the civilian population (conduct of hostilities), or integration of IHL, also referred to as the Law of Armed Conflict or the Law of War, into national armed forces.

Today the ICRC and the US Armed Forces continue to maintain a multi-faceted dialogue that involves a wide-range of issues and, correspondingly, extends to numerous geographic contexts around the world. On one hand, this involves interaction in various operational theatres such as Iraq, Afghanistan, the Philippines and the Horn of Africa. On the other, this interaction involves activities in "non-operational" contexts, mainly in the continental United States, but also in other locations as well. The historical institutionalised integration by the US Government of the law of war into US military doctrine, directives, standing operating procedures and tactics, also promotes the working principles and role of the ICRC in conflict situation. This approach, coupled with the ever-growing joint ICRC—US Armed Forces activities, further underpins the current enhanced dialogue, constructive relationship and better understanding of each other's values.

Dialogue with the US Combatant Commands and Theatre-Level Commands

The ICRC maintains an ongoing dialogue with certain unified combatant commands in order to resolve specific operational issues (e.g. detention, conduct of hostilities) which extend beyond the responsibility of theatre-level commands, as well as to improve mutual understanding. This second aim often includes briefing each other on operations, exchanging information and sharing analysis, such as on humanitarian concerns or on evolving conflict trends in the concerned regions. Meetings are generally at the senior-levels of both institutions, but in some cases also include interaction with staff of the Combatant Commands.

Between 2005 and 2010, the ICRC has increased the frequency of interaction with the US Combatant Commands, conducting meetings with the leadership of CENTCOM, SOUTHCOM, PACOM, EUCOM, AFRICOM, JFCOM and SOCOM. For example, meetings with CENTCOM and SOUTHCOM are generally organised several times per year in order to address operational issues related to the protection of detainees and/or the civilian population in the contexts of Iraq, Afghanistan and Guantanamo; elevating the interaction to one between privileged partners in a confidential dialogue on purely humanitarian issues. Furthermore, in 2008, the ICRC was able to extend its dialogue to the newly established AFRICOM, as well as to SOCOM.

The ICRC also maintains a consistent dialogue with theatre-level commands, like in Afghanistan, principally to resolve specific operational issues relating to the protection of detainees and of the civilian population in terms of conduct of hostilities. The nature of the issues addressed is always contextually dependent, and the more general dialogue focused on the nature of civil-military relations and the respect for "humanitarian space". Such contacts take place at the senior-level of these commands, as well as among staff officers depending on the issues to be addressed.

Pre-Deployment Training and Exercises (MRXs)

Since 2007 the ICRC has prioritised a dialogue with the US Armed Forces not just in theatres of operations (Afghanistan and Iraq), but also more recently prior to deployment to these contexts. This has translated into an enhanced interaction through ICRC involvement in pre deployment exercises, as well as through briefings for US military personnel departing to Iraq and Afghanistan. Such ICRC activities aim first to raise understanding of the ICRC role and operational modalities, as well as humanitarian concerns, in the concerned operational context. This specifically prepares US forces for interaction with ICRC delegates in the context of theatre operations. Secondly, they set the groundwork for future links between the US military units and the ICRC once deployed to the operational context.

The ICRC has participated in an ever-growing number of pre-deployment training exercises and events, at a range of US military facilities both in the continental USA and in Germany, and briefed more than 20 Army Brigade Combat Teams (BCTs) and Marines Expeditionary Units (MEUs). Notably, the following facilities have been engaged by the ICRC:-

(a) US Army National Training Centre (NTC) at Fort Irwin.

(b) US Army Joint-Readiness Training Centre (JRTC) at Fort Polk.

(c) US Army's Joint Multinational Readiness Centre (JMRC) at Hohenfels, Germany.

(d) MRXs involved units deploying to either Iraq or Afghanistan.

(e) USMC training events prior to the deployment of MEF I, MEF II and MEF III. Specific activities have included role-playing the ICRC during MRXs, providing realistic exercise injects depicting contextually adapted scenarios related to ICRC activities, as well as conducting staff briefings on ICRC operations.

The ICRC's involvement at the NTC serves as an example of the added-value of ICRC involvement in pre-deployment exercises (MRX). Since 2007, ICRC has participated in most brigade rotation for units deploying to Iraq or Afghanistan. This interaction means the US Brigade Commanders have practiced meeting the ICRC, are familiar with the detention modalities with the ICRC, and dealt with civil-military issues obliged under the law of war including how the ICRC intervenes on behalf of civilian and military victims of conflict. This investment in quality training illustrates the need for the ICRC and the US forces to understand one other's role prior to deployment to conflict zones.

Over the past three years the ICRC has also participated in a MRX at the JFCOM's Joint Warfare Centre in Suffolk, VA, in order to brief the command and staff officers deploying to the CJTF-HoA. In 2008, the ICRC also reached agreement with the Centre for Law and Military Operations (CLAMO) of the US Army's Judge Advocate General's School to include ICRC as part of CLAMO's pie-deployment training of units rotating into Iraq and Afghanistan.

Dialogue in Military Education and Training

Educational Facilities and Conferences. Over the past several years, the ICRC has worked to intensify its interaction with military educational facilities of the US armed forces, mainly at the intermediate or advanced levels, as well as participate in select conferences sponsored by US Combatant Commands, the Army and the US Marine Corps (USMC). ICRC engagement with military educational facilities aims at improving the understanding of US military personnel of the ICRC, its modus operandi and activities; it also reinforces operational relations between the two institutions through interaction in an academic setting.

Between 2005 and 2010, the ICRC established and/or reinforced relations with a range of the leading US military educational institutions, namely :-

(a) National Defense University (National War College and Industrial College of the Armed Forces).

(b) US Army War College, US Army Command & General Staff College.

(c) US Naval War College.

(d) USMC University, USMC Command & Staff College.

(e) US Army JAG Legal Centre and School (TJAGLCS).

(f) US Army Military Police (MP) School.

(g) US Army School of Engineers.

(h) Joint Special Operations University.

(j) Western Hemisphere Institute of Security Cooperation (WHINSEC)

Specifically, ICRC representatives have participated in courses. seminars and round tables on subject matters in which the ICRC has specific expertise. have lectured on the organisation in general, have conducted briefings on specific ICRC operations or have portrayed the organisation in simulations/exercises in the academic setting. The input is aimed at belier profiling the ICRC in operational environments where it is likely to be one of the key humanitarian actors the military will encounter. Indeed, the CRC always endeavors to tailor its contribution so as to be of relevance to the concerned institution.

The ICRC's involvement at the US Army's JAG Law Centre and School (TJAGLCS) in Charlottesville, VA serves as an example of the ICRC's advanced relationship with the US Army. Extending back some 5 years. The interaction continues to become more dynamic. The multifaceted interaction includes regular ICRC familiarisation presentations at JAG LoW classes, participation by ICRC armed forces delegates in JAG seminars and, since 2007, the organisation of a joint JA-University of Virginia-ICRC annual IHL seminar for concessional staff, think tanks and NGO personnel.

Furthermore, in 2007 an officer from the TJAGLCS attended the first-ever Senior Workshop on International Rules Governing Military Operations (SWIRMO), organised by the ICRC and Swiss Armed Forces. In 2008, the CRC also reached agreement with CLAMO to include ICRC as part of CLAMO's pre-deployment training of units rotating into Iraq and Afghanistan. Beyond military educational institutions, for the past ten years the ICRC has regularly participated as a panel speaker at PACOM's annual Military Law and Operations (MILOPS) Conference. Since 2006, the ICRC has participated as a guest speaker at US Army Europe's (USAREUR) annual Operational Law Continuing Legal Education (CLE) Conference.

Multinational and National Military Exercises

For the past ten years, the ICRC has actively participated in a range of multinational military exercises organised by different US Combatant Commands, although principally in the Asia and Pacific region. ICRC participation in exercises aims at realistically portraying the institution based on the established scenario, as well as raising issues of humanitarian concern linked to the that scenario. It aims to improve the understanding between ICRC representatives and US military personnel, especially in the frame of the military decision- making process. In this sense, the ICRC seeks to add value by realistically presenting the modern challenges faced in situations of conflict and complex emergencies.

The number of exercises to which ICRC has been invited by US armed forces continues to increase. Today, the ICRC regularly participates in the following exercises:-

(a) PACOM-organised exercises in the Asia and Pacific region, namely Cobra Gold (Thailand), Balikatan (Philippines), Talisman Saber (Australia), Khaan Quest (Mongolia), Garuda Shield (Indonesia) and Shaanti Doot-2 (Bangladesh).

(b) SOUTHCOM-organised exercises in the Latin America region, namely PKO-South, PKO-North and Tradewinds.

Negotiations held in 2008 at commander level with JFCOM, the Army Combined Arms Centre (CAC) and the USMC, opened new avenues for interaction and participation of ICRC delegates in some of their major exercises, like the 'Unified Endeavour' series and 'Emerald express'.

Dialogue on Doctrine

In the modern world, doctrine plays an essential role in the effectiveness and professionalism of the armed forces. In this regard, the ICRC places a high-value on the opportunity to offer its perspective and input in the development and revision of US military doctrine on issues related to humanitarian concerns and IHL. Specifically, the ICRC offers its perspectives on and expertise in IHL, as well as its views on the humanitarian impact and consequences of conflict and armed violence. It also works to ensure that the ICRC's mandate and operational modalities are considered in the formulation/revision of US military doctrine.

On the practical level, the ICRC's involvement in the doctrine process is varied, including providing direct written comments on draft documents, participation at seminars that address the doctrine and bilateral discussions with the US military specialists, particularly legal advisers. The added-value of ICRC input for the US military is multi-faceted. Indeed, ICRC offers field- based expertise in the humanitarian dimensions of armed conflict and violence; it also brings long-standing experience on IHL-related topics. Such input can certainly enrich the doctrinal development process.

Between 2005 and 2010, the ICRC provided input and comments in the development or revision of several key US military doctrinal documents, including:-

(a) US Army/USMC FM 3-24/MCWP 3-33.5 Counterinsurgency

(b) JP 3-63 Detainee Operations

(c) JP 3-29 Foreign Humanitarian Assistance

(d) US Army FM 3-07 Stability Operations

(e) PACOM Detention SOPs (developed in the frame of MPAT MNF SOPs) and JFCOM "Rule of Law" Handbook

(f) SOUTHCOM Human Rights Initiative through a series of bilateral consultations on the program's approach, methodology and training tools

Conclusions

Having the ICRC role and mandate understood at all levels of military policy, doctrine, planning and operations is important to both organisations, and this remains the main aim of interaction with the US Armed Forces. The combat experience of the officers and soldiers of the US Armed Forces has facilitated their recognition of the need for neutral, impartial, and independent humanitarian actors, such as the ICRC.

The CRC will strive to maintain and further institutionalise the level of activity with the US Armed Forces in order to consolidate the progress made so far. It is felt that the ICRC and its delegates have many value added activities to offer by interacting closely with the Armed Forces. Overall, there is a shared understanding in the US that the ICRC provides an appropriate early warning system for the humanitarian consequences of US military activity; a rcie envisaged for the ICRC for all armed forces by the Geneva Conventions.

Session IV - Second Paper

21st Century IHL Integration into the Armed Forces: The P5 Countries Experience – (Focusing on the USA and the Russian Federation)

❑ Brigadier General (Retd) William Bowie, Regional Delegate to the Armed and Security Forces of India

General PK Singh, Mr Chairman, ladies and gentlemen, thank you very much for the opportunity to be here and to talk to you a little bit about the activities of the ICRC's Armed Forces Delegate in the Russian Federation. Aleardo spoke to you about America, a country where IHL was well established. Perhaps in the Russian Federation when we started it was not that well established, so what I am going to tell you would be just a little bit more practical than his experiences.

I would first like to talk a little bit about the presence of the ICRC in the Russian Federation, the direction we decided to take and the activities that we are doing. In this, the legal framework is very important to us in what we do, as is the determination of areas of cooperation and how we did this. Finally, I would like to present the actual activities that we have and conclude with a little bit more concerning operational dialogue, about which Aleardo spoke to you. I think you have to understand that what I am going to tell you has been built over a number of years. I was there for four and half years, it was not just when I was there, it was built over a long period of time.

The ICRC started activities in the Russian Federation in 1992 after the break-up of the Soviet Union and because of the Chechnyan revolt. I will not speak too much about Chechnya because I was not there at that time, but at the end of the presentation, I will speak to you a little bit more about South Ossetia and the Georgian-Russian-South Ossetian conflict because I took part in the negotiationS with the Russians in this regard. Let me just say now that at the end of the Chechnyan campaigns and there were two of them, the Russian forces did not come out very well as far as International Humanitarian Law (IHL) is concerned. There are still ongoing cases in international tribunals today where Russia is in court almost every day about atrocities and things that happened at that particular time. So, the Russian Armed Forces at that stage were not perceived as followers of IHL to any great degree. I thought it would be interesting just to tell you that Mr. Paul Castella, who spoke to you this morning on Sri Lanka, was the first armed forces delegate in Moscow at that time. As a successor to the Soviet Union, the Russian Federation is a party to most of the IHL Treaties that were signed by the Soviet Union. However, there are also an IHL related directive and IHL implementation regulations issued in 1989 by the Ministry of Defence that are a legal basis for the implementation of the IHL.

When looking at the IHL related activities over the years, from 1992 right through until I left in 2009, one has to take account the current situation in the country. After the collapse of the Soviet Union, the country was to a certain extent in disorder. We know that the armed forces were in chaos and there were many problems. As I was leaving at the end of 2009, there was a huge reorganisation of the armed forces. Just for interest sake, I think they had in the armed forces at one stage about 300,000 officers; they wanted to cut that down to 100,000, which meant that 200,000 officers were going to lose their jobs and be put onto the street. This makes a very difficult situation for the people involved. As a result, taking into account the activities that led to the current situation in the country, we decided that securing a legal foundation, based on legal norms, for our work within the Ministry of Defence, was really important to us. We needed to establish a procedure so as to determine what kind of cooperation there should be. It is a huge country, if you fly from Moscow to Vladivostok it takes 11 hours and you are still in the same country. The armed forces are 1.2 to 1.3 million, and taking the country's size and armed forces numbers into consideration, we needed, with the limited resources at our disposal, to determine who we were going to talk to and how we were going to do it. We decided that we would conduct IHL dissemination and integration activities, keeping in mind the necessity to have an operational dialogue. Towards the end of this presentation I will talk a little bit about the 2008 conflict in South Ossetia where this operational dialogue was actually very important to the ICRC.

As in India, in Russia contacts with foreigners and foreign organisations have to be approved. We understand this; it is a normal situation in a number of countries. I am a South African and during the time when I was still in the armed forces, it was exactly the same. We could not just go out and talk to foreigners. Therefore, we understood this, and difficulties that this causes for some of the work that we wanted to do. If we wanted to meet somebody, it had to be approved and it could take up to two months to be able to get an appointment. Because of this, we decided that it was very necessary to formalise the relationship about what we were going to do. For this reason, all the planned activities would be included in the annual plan of cooperation. We would go to the Ministry of Defence and sit down with our counterparts in the Russian Federation MoD Main Directorate of for International Military Cooperation and we would talk to them telling them what the ICRC could offer and discussing which activities would be to the best advantage of the Russian Federation. When agreement was reached, the annual plan of cooperation was drawn up and later signed by the Head of Delegation and personally by the Russian Federation Minister of Defence. That gave us a blueprint for the next year of what we could do, without having to get permission for every particular action.

Decisions regarding IHL implementation remain a State responsibility and I am very glad that the Chairman said this. I say again, this is a State responsibility. The States that have signed the Geneva Conventions have agreed that they will implement their provisions. Therefore, it is not an ICRC's responsibility; we are here to offer assistance. We offer assistance as expert advisers on certain aspects of IHL to states in which we work. In order to correctly channel this assistance we established the "Ministry of Defence IHL Integration-Working Group". The group consists of a multi-disciplinary group of officers from the Russian armed forces. We tried to have people from operations, the legal branch, education, training, medical and logistics, in fact everybody who would have something to do with IHL implementation and IHL integration. Why did we put logistics, in there for argument sake ? Well, in the Russian system (and I am not sure about your system), logistics is responsible for Prisoner of War camps and all matters of that nature. The ICRC was part of this working group in an advisory capacity.

The IHL Integration Work Group would discuss IHL integration methods. What was the reason to have a local IHL implementation-working group? Because of the fact that they understand the context in the country much better than outsiders do; know what is possible and what is not possible, know where to go and how to do things, and in the end are the people who can go to higher authority and get approval for what they believe should be done. At meetings of the working group, we would discuss IHL integration methods and IHL integration priorities, because in a country as big as the Russian Federation, you cannot do everything at the same time. We would determine a plan of action for IHL integration in the Russian Federation Armed Forces and as a result, the Russian Ministry of Defence would have an IHL Integration Plan. Then we would look at possible areas of cooperation with the ICRC : Where in this overall integration plan does the ICRC fit and where this assistance could be best utilised with the limited resources that we have to help with this integration ? As you will remember, the Russian Federation MoD Main Directorate for International Military Cooperation had participated in the drawing up of the annual plan of cooperation with the ICRC and gained approval from higher authority for these activities. With this out of the way, we could go ahead and commence our work together. We understood what our responsibilities were, the Russian Federation Ministry of Defence and the Armed Forces understood what we were allowed to do and where we were allowed to go and so we could get down and do some work.

Cooperative activities were various in nature, and to start with, we did many Training of Trainer's Courses. We went to a military base called Senezh (60km outside Moscow) and established a two-week Training of IHL Trainer's course. It is a very interesting course with a large part of it being theoretical, but there were also practical aspects. The practical aspects in the Russian summer were great and it was lovely to go into the field and do them. Unfortunately, I also had to do the practical aspects in the middle of February, in the middle of winter when the plains of Russian would be about minus 25 degrees centigrade. When we started, the ICRC took responsibility for the whole course. The ICRC presented all 10 days as we had all the expertise. Over time until when I left about a year ago, only 25 per cent of the course continued to be undertaken by the ICRC, the rest being presented by Russian officers and Russian academics from various universities.

Because of Russia being such a huge country, it was not possible to get everybody to come to Moscow to attend the course, as half of my budget would have been spent on flying 20 people from Vladivostok to Moscow just to do a course. So, what we did was to take a small training party and travel to the other commands. For example, we went to Vladivostok and travelled around the Caucasus. On these occasions, we would hold one-week Training of Trainer courses for the people from that particular military region. Therefore, the training of trainers was a large part of our activities.

We also ran competitions for trainee officers. At that time, Russia had over 80 officer training schools in the country. We believe that one of the ways to integrate IHL into the armed forces is to get in at the ground level, and lay a solid IHL foundation. What better way to accomplish this than to start with the trainees at officer training schools? For this reason, we established a competition. The competition took place over the period of a week and the trainees were divided into teams of four. There were three days of lectures, one day of practical discussions and one day out in the field where they would go and practice IHL activities. The participants enjoyed the competition and some of them would work hard by themselves to study IHL so that they could get into the team, because in Russia as in many other countries, there is a will to win. As every training school wanted to come first, they would always send the best people to participate and we found that this was a very good way of increasing IHL awareness.

Other activities that we undertook in cooperation with the Russian Federation

MoD included assistance with the revision of doctrine, the discussion of the inclusion of IHL in the curricula of officer training institutions and operational briefing on the mandate and activities of the ICRC. We started the briefing of peacekeeping forces destined for deployment overseas very close to when I was leaving.

Now, let me just talk a little bit about operational dialogue. On the 8th August 2008, Georgia invaded South Ossetia. South Ossetia was supported by the Russian Federation. The Russian Federation reacted to the Georgian attack and moved into South Ossetia from the north. After a short sharp conflict, the Georgians were pushed back into Georgia, with Russia occupying a small part of Georgia before they finally pulled back some weeks later. As I have already stated, this conflict started on 08 Aug 2008.. Because we had established good communication with the Ministry of Defence and the Russian Armed Forces, on the 12th August we managed to get to see the Chief of Staff of the Russian Federation. On the 20th August, because of these negotiations, the ICRC arrived in Tskhinvali *(capital of South Ossetia)* and managed to commence our training activities. A small amount of assistance was given and the ICRC had a mobile hospital on standby for a couple of days, the deployment of which, however, proved unnecessary. In addition, we helped rehabilitate the water and electrical systems of the local hospital. What is of importance here is that 12 days after the conflict, we commenced our operations in South Ossetia and when I left in October 2009, the ICRC was the only humanitarian organisation that had a permanent presence in Tskhinvali. Therefore, I think that one of the most important aspects was that we managed to successfully liaise with the authorities and knew whom to talk to. As a result, when this unfortunate situation occurred we entered into dialogue got down on the ground and were able to help the people that needed to be helped as quickly as possible. Normally, among these were people were not part of the conflict and they just happened to be in the wrong place at the wrong time. In my presentation, I have tried to be practical about what we did in the Russian Federation and to give you an idea as to how this was achieved.

I thank you very much for your attention.

Session IV - Discussion (Q & A)

Issue Raised

The way I see IHL, it is a lot of '*theory*' and 'sermonising' about what all should be done. It is important that all the countries who are signatories should follow it. For example, Pakistan would not follow IHL, and there is nothing the international community can do, to compel it to conform to International norms in this regard. What are the implications of IHL for such countries who just do not come on line?

Response

The implementation of IHL is essentially a national responsibility. Since the ICRC role is to assist the countries, it confines itself to rendering such help wherever it can. If the country concerned does not abide by the rules it is regrettable but such aberrations do not fall under ICRC's jurisdiction. The ICRC can do nothing about it. It does, however, try to ensure that people understand what is right, but, when they deliberately decide not to act according to law, then it is a problem, which is out of ICRC's jurisdiction.

Issue Raised

Whenever, there has been an earthquake or natural disaster e.g. in Haiti, Columbia or Guatemala, lot of problems are faced in the initial three to four days in dealing with humanitarian aspects to provide succour to the affected people expeditiously. *How can the ICRC help in coordinating the relief effort to* ensure that, firstly, the material needs are identified correctly and the donors deliver the relief material at the right place so that the aid is rendered efficiently and effectively without losing precious time?

Response

(a) As far as coordinating International aid in case of sudden disaster, it is always a difficult situation because they happen so quickly e.g., the Haiti earthquake made so many people homeless in about a minute and five seconds. In such cases, *firstly,* the 'work' has to be 'assessed' to decide, what items are required and from whom, and whether certain things can be purchased. Then there is a need to coordinate between colleagues to come to an understanding as to who is going to fulfil the various responsibilities and how. There is no point in five aircraft reaching at the same place where they are not required and with the same material.

(b) The first 24 to 48 hours are the most critical and most difficult period and that is the time when all the organisations have to work very hard. At the ICRC Headquarters, an emergency reaction team is called out whenever such situations happen. They are the persons who are empowered to decide what should happen and when it should happen. They can call experts from various fields of the ICRC and dispatch them within 24 hours to the area of the crisis. They can gauge, what is required and get back to the headquarters with the right information so that the right aid can be sent at the right time. For example, *there is* a sub-delegation of the ICRC in Kabardino-Balkaria in the city of Nalchik, which covers these aspects in respect of North Ossetia, Chechnya and Dagestan. A lot of relief assistance was given in Nalchik.

Issue Raised

As a matter of policy, the ICRC dos not reveal its communications with the government to maintain confidentiality; that is fair and quite understandable. But in case a country does not follow the rules of the game and does not adhere to these provisions, w*ould it help if the ICRC makes their findings public, something like what the Human Rights Commission does?* That would put a certain amount of moral pressure on the defaulting countries to fall in line; specially if the details are published, after warning them suitably over a period of time.

Response

(a) This is a fair question. The ICRC's confidentiality is not '*absolute*'. There are situations where if certain conditions are not met the ICRC would go public and actually make public certain information regarding the region. But this must really be done in a last resort situation only. Since the ICRC actually works on the ground, it understands when such a situation has developed, to provide humanitarian aid to persons who desperately need to be helped. There are ways through which people, who matter, can be impacted upon.

(b) However, we do know that going public would at times hamper ICRC action. That is why, as a policy framework, a bilateral confidential approach with the concerned governments is preferred. The ICRC prefers to take a pragmatic view for continuing legal access to the government.

(c) In a situation when the ICRC has reached the conclusion, that doing so would not harm the persons concerned and the bilateral avenue has been exhausted, there are situations where public denunciation through headlines in newspapers may be resorted to. However, the ICRC prefers a bilateral approach, even though often it is frustrating.

Chairman's Closing Remarks

Two significant points have been raised during this session.

Firstly, one is about the '*coordination of the relief effort*' in emerging situations. Without going into details, it would suffice for me to confirm that there are enough agencies available to coordinate ICRC relief work on an emergency basis. Of course, much depends on the nature and impact of the disasters in different situations. I have seen it happen in many areas and the system has worked quite well to meet the needs of the affected people.

The second point was: *How do you bring the violators of IHL to book?* Countries continuously violate the accepted IHL norms. How they can be made accountable, is a question. It would be appropriate for me to suggest that Mr Stamm may answer this question in his concluding remarks.

I would now conclude this session by saying that '*ideas*' *and* '*debates*' on *observance* of HR and IHL should include the Armed Forces leadership. They are the ones who matter most in observance of IHL during armed conflicts. Therefore, they must be invited to reflect their views and practical difficulties in adhering to IHL norms.

In this context, IHL has faced some criticism from certain quarters that it does not anticipate the challenges involved in fighting '*modern terrorism*', where motivated and well-armed trans-national armed groups enjoy the patronage and backing of the states that use them to further own interests. In such situations, some states consider existing laws as a hindrance and propose that when '*law*' *and* '*material reality*' clash, it is the law, which must give way, to facilitate successful operations to overcome the advantages enjoyed by non-state actors. I think IHL should make provisions to cover such new forms of conflicts. This perhaps calls for the expansion of the 'Concept of Armed Conflicts' or expansion of the scope of application of IHL beyond armed conflicts.

In the future, rapid technological advances would throw up new challenges for safeguarding human rights and the observance of IHL. For example, the use of directed energy weapons and cyber warfare can freeze transportation, electric supply and communication networks. This would have a huge impact on the civilian population- though the collateral damage may not be so intended. These may be termed as military issues but they could have indirect consequences. The uniformed organisations have to be involved in all such ongoing debates to keep abreast with the emerging challenges in modern day conflicts.

In the morning session, the 'continued relevance' of the IHL was emphasised by the Director, USI. I fully endorse that assertion. I am convinced that IHL has to rise to the new challenges in the shape of new wars and new threats. My basic understanding is that IHL is fine and its boundaries are properly drawn. It maintains a respectful balance for meeting the interests of state securely, individual security and civil liberties. IHL is effective, like all other laws, when properly implemented.

Thank you very much ladies and gentlemen. I would like to convey my special thanks to both the panellists and Brigadier General Bowie, who gave us a very insightful presentation on Russia.

Concluding Remarks

Mr François Stamm, HoRD of the ICRC in India

Lieutenant General PK Singh, PVSM,AVSM (Retd), Director USI

Concluding Remarks

❑ Mr François Stamm, HoRD of the ICRC in New Delhi

After a long and very interesting day, I am grateful for your attention and active participation in the discussion. My mind goes back to the time when the idea of holding an IHL seminar came up between Lt Gen PK Singh, Director, USI and Mr Brian Donkin. Thereafter, came a regular exchange, and the idea of introducing the way the ICRC works with a number of different armies – especially the P-5 Nations and the bringing in of some credible operational expertise and experiences from the conflicts in Sri Lanka, Afghanistan and so on.

I am very grateful for your support, for your work and for welcoming us, not only, as I said in my introductory remarks, to this event but also to the regular activities organised by USI. I would like to thank Major General PJS Sandhu, who has played a very important role in making this happen, and worked tirelessly for this event to be successful. At the ICRC, we have Mr Ashish Bhatia who has worked a lot behind the scenes to achieve this.

Just briefly, let me be candid to tell you that the ICRC's intentions are not entirely innocent. It is true that we would like to have a better access and a better interaction with the Indian Armed Forces. We hope that, by showing you what we are doing with other major powers, and the Russian model, to be honest, is what we would like to achieve here. We want to be transparent and predictable, and through discussion allow a sound relationship to develop.

We hope we can convince the decision makers by having the necessary meetings, which will, hopefully, increase our cooperation and exchange. We feel we have the ability to make a significant contribution. We meet many people within Indian society and the Indian Armed Forces who share the same view. I am optimistic for the future. I think we are moving in the right direction. We hope that, with your support, and with events like this, we will reach a common objective. We think, we can bring something to the table on these issues and, very importantly, we can learn something from you.

As the Head of the Delegation in New Delhi for two years now, one of my main visions is not only to work to provide services, to visit prisoners in J&K and other places, but also to take back to Geneva the views of New Delhi and the voice of India.

We realise now, that our role is becoming much more important. This is the right time for us to stop looking at our western egocentric views. We need to integrate more views from Beijing, New Delhi and South Africa, and we should also have a real exchange of ideas.

Therefore, in this situation, I look forward to receiving cooperation from the Indian Armed Forces in our endeavours. The Indian Armed Forces have terrific experience, being a very powerful Army and I am sure we have plenty of things to learn from you.

Thank you for your support. That has indeed been very helpful in achieving our common objectives.

Concluding Remarks

❑ Lieutenant General PK Singh,PVSM,AVSM (Retd), Director, USI

At the outset I must thank François Stamm for the support he provided to us in putting this seminar together. As he said, before our first meeting, we discussed the issue in-house and concluded that the ICRC wants to have a tie up and linkages with the Indian Armed Forces. We realised that the way we were going about it previously, we would not achieve very much.

To begin with, we needed to understand the Indian Armed Forces' perception on the issues that concern the ICRC; and how they would benefit from such a tie up and linkages between the two. Based on that assessment, we had discussions with our counterparts in the Indian Armed Forces. We told them of the need to know, how the ICRC functions in strife-affected countries, especially in countries like Sri Lanka and Afghanistan, where their security forces and International forces are engaged in counter insurgency and counter terrorism operations to safeguard respective national interests.

You were kind enough to get your delegates to interact with us and we did learn and understand the way you work. A presentation like this actually tells the interested people about the ICRC's role and how its delegates work on the ground between the various parties involved in an armed conflict.

We also wanted to know the kind of interaction the ICRC wanted with the Indian Armed Forces, especially against the background of their similar interactions with the American and Russian Armed Forces. What did the ICRC learn from those interactions and what do such tie ups mean to the parties involved in a conflict?

In this context, I would like to flag an issue for the future by asking: Did the ICRC go along with the British Forces into Ireland? This is to know, if the ICRC makes a difference between and internal deployment of the Armed Forces by a country for its Internal Security, where the ICRC may or may not have a role; and the other type i.e. of International deployment, like the American Armed Forces coming into Afghanistan or Iraq. Does the ICRC have different connotations in such characteristically distinct armed conflicts? It would also interest me to know that if the ICRC was in China, would they take you to Tibet – when they are having problems in Tibet or to Tianamen etc? I think we need to be clear on certain issues, especially when there is an internal dimension to a conflict and where a country's armed forces are engaged in support of the civil administration.

There is a large distance to be travelled before the ICRC can have an 'Observer' status to understand how the Indian Armed Forces work. For this, you have to go step by step. In this context, I would like to point out that even the Indian Army, Navy and the Air Force do not attend all of each other's war games and exercises conducted by them. However, I would like to say that whenever you decide to do any research on the Indian Armed Forces, do include the Indian institutions and think tanks to understand the issues in the right perspective. The point that I am making is that when you are having such discussions and giving your recommendations regarding the Indian Armed Forces, do take somebody from India on board to give the Indian viewpoint, because of India's experience in tackling complex internal conflicts and Peacekeeping in international armed conflicts.

Some people may be feeling that we are already partners because we are discussing these issues together. Such discussions with think tanks do help in getting significant inputs about the Indian Armed Forces, which are in the public domain. In this sense, the USI looks forward to such interactions with the ICRC because we both benefit from these. I am confident that next time, there will be even more representation from the Indian Armed Forces because of their conviction that there is merit in talking to you.

In the end, all that remains for me to do is to thank the ICRC, and more importantly all the four eminent Chairmen and the panellists and every single person who has been here since this morning, and specially the large group that have stayed put from morning until now. We at the USI enjoyed having you with us and we always look forward to your participation.

I thank you once again and wish you the very best.

